W9-CLZ-008

Alabama Stitch Book

Projects and Stories Celebrating Hand-Sewing, Quilting, and Embroidery for Contemporary Sustainable Style

For Zach and Maggie

Natalie Chanin
with Stacie Stukin

Photography by Robert Rausch

STC Craft/A Melanie Falick Book

Stewart, Tabori & Chang
New York

Contents

Living Arts

In the year 2000, I returned home to Florence, Alabama, to create a collection of clothing that came to be known as Project Alabama. Although I had been gone from Alabama for more than 22 years, I quickly settled into the community where my grandparents had lived. Just outside of Florence, where Mud Road meets the Old Savannah Highway, Lovelace Crossroads is just one of the many intersections of country roads that lie along the edge of rolling, dark red cotton fields and stretch out beneath the endless blue North Alabama sky.

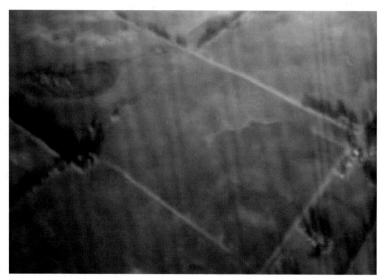

Lovelace Crossroads: Latitude 34° 47′ N and
Longitude 87° 75′ W from 678 ft, 4th day of January

This beautiful landscape, at the foothills of the Appalachian Mountains, provided the backdrop for Project Alabama, which became known for elaborately embellished, hand-sewn garments that were sold in stores around the world.

At its zenith, Project Alabama enlisted the craftsmanship of approximately 200 artisans—whom we called "stitchers." These artisans lived and worked within a three-hour radius of my small, three-bedroom, ranch-style home at Lovelace Crossroads. The work of the Project Alabama stitchers was revered by fashion insiders and the public at large. The business model, which used a cottage industry-style approach, was touted by business magazines and called "the way of the future."

In the fall of 2006, Project Alabama ceased operations at Lovelace Crossroads. And though my journey with Project Alabama came to an end, a new company called Alabama Chanin grew out of the fertile ground that I nurtured for all those years.

Alabama Chanin is still headquartered in Florence, and we continue to design clothing using recycled fabrics, mainly 100 percent cotton jersey, while employing age-old techniques to produce them. We also enlist the local quilters and seamstresses who grew up—like me—learning to sew at the feet of grandmothers, mothers, and aunts.

For generations, creation was part of these women's everyday lives. Making beautiful and delicious things that enriched our world—cobblers and pies, everyday clothes and Sunday best, tatted lace and embroidered pillowcases, strawberry preserves, fresh tomato juice, summer bonnets and pickles—was part of their daily routine. They made quilts, knitted afghans, baked bread, "put up" peas, and stitched beautiful prom dresses—like the blue gown I've loved for as long as I can remember. Every time I look at it, I can imagine my grandmother's fine long fingers meticulously fitting row after row of lace so that my aunt could be the "belle of the ball" for that one special night.

Today when I sit and look at the beautiful textiles that I have inherited, I see that the women and men who raised me were artisans in their own right. They created sustainable products by using the materials that were readily available to them in the community. Even though these creations enhanced our lives immeasurably, they were never considered anything extraordinary and the people who made them were extremely humble about their work.

At Alabama Chanin, we consider their work to be extraordinary, and we try to reclaim a time when products were made by hand by skilled artisans who played an esteemed role in their communities. Unfortunately, these domestic arts, which I prefer to call living arts, are fading as our lives get busier and busier and we rely more and more on store-bought goods. That's one reason we use these traditional crafting traditions, but we always strive to give them a contemporary context.

These living arts have been passed down by oral histories through generations of women and men—connecting us to our roots, our past, our community, and consequently to our present. Living arts are an essential part of the social fabric of our communities—like planting seeds, reaping the fruits of our labors, and preserving our food. Such traditions are the backbone of what makes a community a home, and preserving them ensures that future generations can enjoy the same quality of life with the same attention to detail, function, and beauty.

Working this way takes time. Some call this approach "Slow Design," which means embracing the long-term view over the short-term gain by using age-old techniques to create products that celebrate strong design principles for modern living. You can say my work harkens back to time-honored stitching traditions, but I'm still a modern woman who wants versatility and freedom. I need clothes that move with me, not clothes that determine my movements. And when I look around my home, I want to see products that remind me that good design can be a part of everyday living.

The book you're holding is a testament to that desire. It was born years ago when I first began designing with these traditional techniques. I quickly realized that I needed to develop a common language to describe the methods I was using. One night while working on this problem, I sat down and hand-wrote a collection of notes, instructions, and simple illustrations and laid down some ground rules about how I would use them. This original "Stitch Book" helped me innovate new ways of working and provided the foundation for a wide variety of products.

I've come a long way since that first handwritten "road map" to stitching. Along my way, I've had the luxury of being surrounded by talented people and also the joy of collecting a lot of tips, treats, and tales. There have been

many turns along this path, but I'm happy to be able to finally share my experiences in the hope that we can all find a way to sustain our rich traditions.

Natalie

The Office at Lovelace Crossroads

Row 1 - Hand-sewn coat, My grandmother and friends on cotton-picking day, circa 1930s, Picked cotton field, Vintage quilts.

Row 2 - Cotton T-shirts, Cypress Creek, Interior weaving room, Ashcraft Cotton Mills, circa 1910 (W.L. McDonald Collection, The University of North Alabama, photographer unknown), Cotton ready for ginning.

Row 3 - Ashcraft Cotton Mills company picnic, circa 1910 (W.L. McDonald Collection, The University of North Alabama, photographer unknown), Cotton bolls, One of my early designs, Cypress Mills, circa 1885 (W.L. McDonald Collection, The University of North Alabama, photographer, Adolphe Hovelle).

CHAPTER 1 | Cotton

Cotton has been part of the everyday vernacular of this community for generations. In the early fall, the smell of ripe cotton fills the air with its seductive, woodlike scent. For some, that scent is reminiscent of prosperity. For others, it conjures up memories of backbreaking work; yet others think about the cotton and textile mills that were the heart of this community. To this day, our county is one of the state's top ten producers of cotton, and it's hard to mention cotton without someone having a personal connection to the fiber that has a long, and sometimes ugly, history.

Gloria Faye Davis, a former textile worker, had worked in cotton textile factories for 34 years. She was raised on a farm and says with dry wit, "I've been on my knees a bunch picking cotton." Her humor alludes to the harsh physical labor that cotton picking requires. It can be painful for your knees, your back, your hands. Brenda Harrison, an artisan whose embroidery stitches are breathtakingly even and concise, is a Choctaw Indian. The Choctaws were among the first people to settle in Alabama, and, on her reservation, everyone grew up picking cotton. "It just was that way," she says. When my Aunt Elaine was a teenager, she used to pick cotton in Jim Mills' field because "that's where all the cute boys were." For her, it was a part-time job that provided extra spending money. For Mr. Mills and men like him, it was a livelihood.

Mr. Mills is now in his nineties. He still wears denim overalls, and his face shows off years spent out in the fields. Even though his farm swelled to two thousand acres in the 1970s, his memories are mostly of hard work to feed his family. "There wasn't anything else to do around here except farm cotton. It was a rough life. You had to work day and night to make a living." In the 1930s, he used mules to plow the land. Then they planted the cotton seed and painstakingly hand-weeded the fledgling plants to allow them to blossom unfettered by the damaging weeds. "We didn't use chemicals back then," he recalls. "It was hard work and all done by hand. We picked the bolls by hand and then put them in a sack." That was a time when there was a cotton gin every three to five miles that would separate the fiber from the seed and prepare it to be used to make yarn and then fabric. This sort of devotion to the red, rich earth is part of the folklore for farmers who built up the cotton legacy of the South.

In this part of the country, the cotton industry was built on slave labor. Pietra Rivoli, in her 2005 book, *The Travels of a T-Shirt in the Global Economy*, writes that by the outbreak of the Civil War, the South was producing a billion pounds of cotton a year. That comprised two-thirds of the world's cotton production. This could not have happened without plantations where the physical hardship fell on slaves and later sharecroppers, who spent hours in the blazing heat, dragging a cotton-filled sack behind them as they hand-picked the sharp bolls that brought blood to their fingers.

The Civil War ended slavery, but it also devastated the cotton industry in this community when Union soldiers burned down the two existing cotton factories. As the town of Florence began the process of rebuilding, cotton remained an important economic force, says William L. McDonald, now 79 years old. The author of several books on Florence, Mr. McDonald is the historian of our city, which was founded in 1818 along the Tennessee River (and named by an Italian surveyor after his favorite city). On many afternoons, Mr. McDonald can be found upstairs in a sunny spot of the downtown library, surrounded by colleagues who pore over old news accounts. "Some of the first cotton fabric production in the country happened right here in east Florence," he says.

This community expanded during America's burgeoning Industrial Revolution in the 1890s, and mill villages began to sprout up around these factories. Until recently you could see remnants of this time along Sweetwater Creek. There, a factory building with tall windows and a faded brick facade recalls a time when men, women, and children worked inside for meager wages making union suits, men's underwear, and undershirts. "The workers barely made a living," Mr. McDonald says. "They worked ten to twelve hours a day, six days a week. They lived in homes owned by the company; they shopped at company stores.

They really didn't have much of a chance to get ahead." But the promise of work kept families coming to Florence and to other Southern cities. Their productivity paid off. By the mid-1930s, according to Rivoli, 75 percent of the cotton-yarn spindles in America were in the South.

During the Depression, many of these cotton mills suffered along with rest of the country. Most closed down. It was a time in our community when women like my neighbor, Mrs. Evelyn Killen, 89, had to rely on what they had on hand to clothe and feed their families. When she talks about these times, it is not with bitterness but with a practical, matter-of-fact tone. She once told me, "Times were hard, and we didn't have much. I guess you could say that we were poor, but we didn't know it. We had enough of the necessities, and we did all that we could to get by. You know, we used everything. There was no such thing as a garbage can. I don't even think that we had a word for it. We had a slop bucket to feed scraps to the hogs, but the rest was re-used. Flour sacks made our dresses and the scraps made the quilts that kept us warm in the winter."

That was the beauty of using and re-using what you had; it was a necessity that fueled a unique creativity. It's amazing what you can discover when you're forced to use what's on hand. For example, sacks that contained flour, sugar, salt, and grains became coveted items for farm wives, who used the 100-percent cotton bags printed with different floral patterns to make clothes, quilts, toys, underwear, pillowcases, and just about anything else that required fabric.

"I was always glad when we went to buy flour sacks, and I got to pick out the pattern," recalls Clois Manchester fondly. Mrs. Manchester, 90, is still an avid quilter. When she was young, she says nothing went to waste. One of her sisters had a knack for turning their father's worn-out felt farming hats into clothes for their dolls. And after the cotton harvest, she and her sisters and mother would retrieve the "scrap cotton" that was left on her daddy's field. These last little bits that continued to grow after the cotton harvest would be spread out on a sheet and whipped with switches to separate the seeds from the fiber. I was told once by Mrs. Allen, a long-time quilter, that "they would just whip and whip and that cotton would just fly up in the air, all fluffy. It looked just like snow." This fluffy scrap cotton was then spread out evenly and used as batting for their beautiful quilts.

Thread was also a luxury for women in families like Mrs. Manchester's. Since money was tight, they would unravel the thread from food sacks to use later in sewing projects. Especially in demand was red thread, which was hard to find and expensive. One ingenious technique used to obtain the coveted red was to unweave the popular Red Man Tobacco pouches. Today, if you see an old quilt with red thread in these parts, it likely came from one of those pouches.

Quilts were a necessity for warmth, and the making of them was a joy. At the end of the summer when all the vegetables were put up from the garden, ladies would get together and quilt. "There was so much work to do over the course of the summer days that they did not get much of a chance to visit," explains Barbara Broach, the director of our local art museum, The Kennedy-Douglass Center. "When the fields would die back, the houses would come to life. It was a gathering of the whole community. They would all come and bring food and their kids and their stories, and those ladies would sit around that quilt and exchange stories and gossip. Then at lunch, they would take a break and have chicken and field peas and biscuits and all the good Southern cooking that you could think of."

It's hard to imagine that a culture without a word for garbage can in the 1930s and 1940s has become a culture that throws so much away today—our water bottles, plastic bags, clothing, and the cotton T-shirts that I've chosen to use in my work. My home of Florence, Alabama, once called itself the "T-shirt Capital of the World." T-shirt manufacturing kept this community employed; and, like most things around here, it's a story that is tied to cotton.

Alice Harris, author of *The White T* (1996), explains that the T-shirt became popular after World War II, when American soldiers returned home with military-issued crewneck, short-sleeved jersey shirts. The army recognized that those T-shirts protected against sun and bugs; were comfortable; and, in trench warfare when things got wet, dried quickly. *Life* magazine noted the allure of the piece in its 1951 proclamation that the T-shirt "has gone high fashion...appearing on city streets and country club porches—and even at formal dances."

But it was the hippie culture of the 1960s and 1970s that shuttled the T-shirt into the modern age. It was no longer reserved for those looking to front a Jimmy Dean Rebel-Without-a-Cause facade. Instead, the popularity of personalizing T-shirts with tie-dye and screen-printing signaled the rise of casual wear and the desire to state your credo on your back. Harris writes that in 1978 alone, more than 500 million T-shirts were sold in the United States.

My friend Marigail Mathis was part of that boom. In 1972, she helped her family open Lexington Fabrics in Florence. "We went into the clothing business because we heard T-shirts were the coming thing," she says from the clothing shop she now owns in town. "We heard T-shirts were going from underwear to outerwear, and we thought that was amazing. And it was. It took off like a rocket."

Lexington Fabrics was one of many T-shirt manufacturers and printers in the area. There was also Salem Screen South and Tee Jays Manufacturing. At its peak, Lexington Fabrics alone employed eleven hundred people and made millions of pounds of jersey fabric a year. "In some cases we had three generations of families working with us, and they were all like family," Marigail recalls.

But things began to change in the mid-1990s. Technological advances coupled with competition from overseas for cheaper labor caused layoffs and job eliminations in the textile industry all over the United States. The passage of the North American Free Trade Agreement (NAFTA), which lifted trade restrictions and allowed open-door trade policies, only exacerbated the situation. In Florence, it wasn't just about T-shirts. There were many other jeans-wear and clothing factories in the area. Since NAFTA's passage in 1994, twenty-seven garment factories have shut down in our region alone.

I came back to Alabama when this scenario was unfolding. As I began to interview stitchers, I heard all kinds of stories about women and men who worked in factories for decades, only to be left without jobs. As for Lexington

Fabrics, they closed their doors in 2003. Marigail is sad when she talks about that time. "We hired the best advisors in the business to figure out how we could stay open," she says. "We knew it was coming, but it was a long, heartbreaking goodbye, and every employee we had to let go was like a gash in our hearts."

Marigail's story illustrates why it's hard these days to find jobs like the one Clois Manchester had working in a textile factory for 26 years. That job not only enabled her to support her family; it also allowed her to retire with a good pension. Manchester's granddaughter Michelle Rupe Eubanks, a reporter for the *Times Daily* in Florence, wrote a story in 2005 about the demise of the local textile industry and the jobs it provided. Michelle's expertise has helped me tell this story, and when she talks about the closing of companies like Tee Jays and Lexington Fabrics, she says their disappearance reminds us that the T-shirt industry is gone from Florence, probably forever. "So many people worked there. It was part of our culture," she observes while sipping her favorite sweet tea.

Michelle points out that most of the cotton grown in our area today is actually shipped to China, where T-shirts are manufactured and then shipped back to the United States. "Cotton has an odd way about it," she says. First cotton manufacturing left England and ended up in New England. From there it moved to the South. Now it's gone to Mexico and China. "I've always said cotton is fickle. It just picks up and goes where it wants."

But in the South we must take ownership of cotton for all its good and its bad. I have made my steps towards ownership by taking old, recycled T-shirts (many of which were made right here in my community), cutting them apart, and sewing them back together again—that is my small way of moving beyond our past in order to make a fresh start.

CHAPTER 2 | Supplies

Getting started is as simple as collecting the supplies needed to make that proverbial first step. For as long as people have been sewing, their supplies have basically been the same—needle, thread, fabric, and scissors (or knives or sharp flint in the case of our earliest sewing ancestors). Over time, each of us develops a system for keeping supplies accessible and organized. My grandmother kept her sewing notions in an oval, yellow wicker box and stored her neatly folded fabrics in the closet of the "lavender room," named for the color of its walls. With vaulted eves, the closet was the size of a small attic, and I remember spending long afternoons in there, hidden from the world.

I inherited that yellow wicker notions box from my grandmother, and, like her, I keep needles, thread, and embroidery scissors on an old ceramic plate on my work table. But rather than storing my fabrics hidden in the closet, I keep them out in the open, stacked neatly and sorted by color or project on stainless-steel restaurant racks. On these shelves, I also keep wicker baskets for ribbons, trims, and other supplies, so everything is organized and accessible.

In this chapter, you'll find recommendations for gathering your supplies for the projects in this book. There's information about how to pick your cotton-jersey fabric and colors, and recommendations for needles, thread, scissors, and other notions. And scattered in between are tips and some specific techniques to help you as you get started.

Cotton Jersey

In the lectures and workshops I give, I try to show how it's possible to create a multitude of diverse products with something as simple and basic as cotton jersey—the fabric most T-shirts are made of. I always find that people are interested to learn that, on a microscopic level, cotton fibers look like little squiggles. And it's the nature of these cotton fibers that makes the fabric inherently soft and absorbent.

Cotton-jersey fabric is manufactured on knitting machines and can be made from 100-percent cotton fibers or from a blend of cotton and other fibers. We use exclusively 100-percent cotton-jersey fabric, which comes in a variety of weights. Lightweight jersey, often used for designer T-shirts that drape naturally along the body's contours, is soft, almost sheer, and has a light, airy feel because it's knitted with a very fine-gauge yarn on very small needles. By contrast, heavyweight jersey, knitted with a heavier yarn on medium to large needles, has a thick, durable feel and is used for sports clothing and other heavy-duty garments.

I prefer to use something in-between sheer and heavy jerseys—a medium-weight cotton jersey, which is stable, feels sturdy, and is versatile in terms of its uses. And, when possible, I choose cotton jersey made from organic cotton fibers and encourage everyone else to do the same.

Choosing Your Cotton Jersey

You can get cotton jersey by recycling old T-shirts or buying it new at the fabric store. The best jersey is made from fibers that feel smooth, soft, and pliable when you touch them. Avoid cheap, thin jersey, which can pill, or produce small "balls" on the surface when well worn, and look dirty. Cheaper jerseys are also prone to getting holes and wearing out more quickly then better-quality jerseys. When recycling vintage T-shirts, be careful that the cotton has not worn too thin because a fabric worn thin will soon become threadbare or even develop holes.

Whether you recycle cotton jersey T-shirts or buy new fabric, make sure to wash it before you start working with it to ensure that it doesn't change color or shrink and that the dye doesn't run. This is especially important when working with red fabric, which has a tendency to bleed and/or fade.

Over time you'll come to know intuitively which jersey works best for your projects. When making small items like a headband (page 103) or flower bouquet (page 135), you may want to choose recycled T-shirts. When working on a larger project like a tablecloth (page 125) or skirt (pages 149 and 165), you may want to buy cotton-jersey yardage (either flat or in a tube) to avoid spending a lot of time piecing and stitching together enough deconstructed T-shirts to get the necessary amount of fabric.

Thread

There are many types of thread, and it's important to choose wisely. For most purposes, I use what's called buttonhole, carpet, and craft thread (named for its various uses), which is thicker than ordinary sewing thread. For basting necklines and armholes before constructing garments, I use standard all-purpose thread.

Buttonhole, carpet, and craft thread is made with a polyester core surrounded by cotton and is one of the strongest threads available. You can wash it over and over again without it breaking or wearing. Its thickness is ideal for embroidered embellishment, and its polished finish helps prevent it from weakening as you pull it through your fabric while sewing. This strong thread only comes in nine colors; see right for tips on choosing a color.

While it's very tempting to collect those beautiful, old wooden spools from your grandmother's sewing box, thread does get old and brittle. My friend Butch Anthony wondered why all his patched overalls kept falling apart after he hand-stitched them and wore them a few times. It turned out that he was using antique thread that he bought at a local auction. To prevent such mishaps, do a simple break test by holding a strand of thread and tugging on it to see if it breaks easily. If it does, splurge on a new spool!

Why Thread Knots

While working on one of the elaborate evening gowns in our collection for more than a month, I had plenty of time to think about why thread tangles. Here's what I learned:

When thread is made, microscopic, squiggly cotton fibers are combed in the same direction into two strands, each called a ply. Then one of these plies is twisted to the right (in an "S" twist), while the other strand is twisted to the left (in a "Z" twist). The two plies are then twisted around each other as tightly as possible, so that, when released, they relax, "expand," and join around one another to create a single strand of thread. The tension between the two plies explains not only why your thread doesn't fray but also why it tends to knot sometimes as you're sewing. To reduce the excess tension, "love" your thread, as explained at right.

Choosing Your Thread Color

My Aunt Elaine taught home economics for over thirty years, and she once passed an old tip to me—if you can't find thread in your fabric's exact shade, buy a shade darker because it sews in lighter.

In my stitching, I use two different and equally valid thread options—matching thread and contrasting thread: Matching thread should match the base fabric's color as closely as possible. If you can't match a color easily, try to match the color's tone. Do this by laying out your thread options on your fabric, squinting, and looking for the thread that blends with your fabric in the most understated way. Matching thread yields elegant, subtle results.

Thread that contrasts with the top fabric color shows off your stitches. A lighter contrasting thread lends a "rougher" look since the stitches themselves become a graphic element. By contrast, stitches in a darker thread tend to merge more quietly with the shape they define.

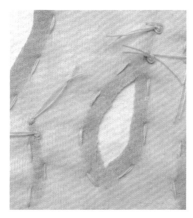

Thread matching the fabric color (see left) produces understated results, while contrasting thread yields more graphic results (see right).

"Loving" Your Thread

"Loving" your thread infuses the work with kind intentions, but it's also a very practical step that removes excess thread tension and prevents pesky knotting.

Here's how to love your thread: Cut the thread twice as long as the distance from your fingers to your elbow. Thread your needle, and pull the two thread ends, so they're the same length. Hold the doubled thread between your thumb and index finger, and run your fingers along it from the needle to the end of the loose tails while saying, "This thread is going to sew the most beautiful garment ever made. The person who wears this garment (use his or her name if you know it) will wear it in health and happiness; it will bring joy and laughter."

Continue loving that thread, wishing it all the good that you can think of, and running it through your fingers again and again. What you're actually doing is working the tension out of the tightly twisted thread with rubbing, pressure, and the natural oils in your fingers. In the process, you've also taken a moment to calm the tension in your mind, concentrate on the task at hand, and add just a little bit of love to your garment or project. Now you're ready to tie off your knot (see page 40) and start sewing.

Measuring, Marking, and Pattern-Making Tools

Rulers

I recommend transparent plastic rulers with a grid printed on them because they're wider than standard rulers and their grid lines help you work in straight lines. I like to use a flexible 6" ruler when I draw designs or stitch. I use sturdier 18" or 24" rulers when I'm making patterns and cutting fabric and need more stability.

Tailor's Chalk

Tailor's chalk is a great tool for novice stitchers to use for marking a stitching line to follow (see page 35). Always test your chalk color on your project fabric before you commit to it, since some colors work better and brush away more easily than others on a particular fabric.

Disappearing-Ink Pens

Disappearing-ink pens are good for small tasks like marking patterns, transferring stencils in small areas, and drawing shapes for cutting out appliqués. Some pens use an ink that disappears when you rub the fabric with a damp cloth; others use an ink that disappears on its own over a short time (so don't delay once you've marked your fabric). Whatever brand or type of pen you choose, always test it on a discreet area on your fabric before using it.

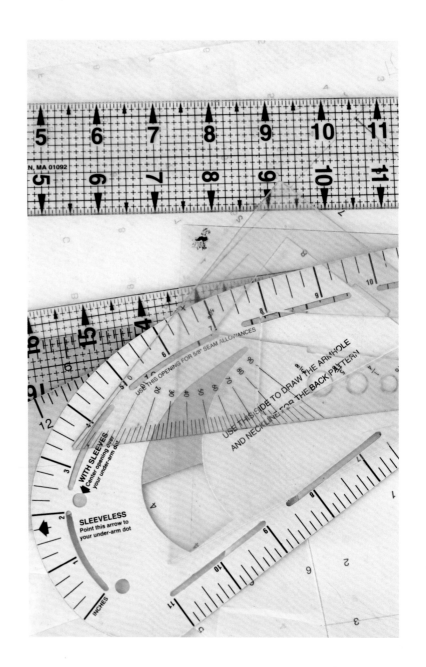

Paper

Paper is a necessity for accomplishing a wide variety of sewing and stenciling tasks. Here are brief descriptions of the different kinds of paper you might use for the projects in this book.

Available at fabric stores, lightweight **pattern paper** comes with a grid of dots or numbers on one side (see photo at left). This grid is particularly helpful when making patterns because the dots provide a guide for pattern lines. I use pattern paper to prepare patterns; and when I'm sure that everything is right, I transfer the cut pattern pieces to heavier-weight card stock.

Butcher paper is white paper that is usually waxed on one side and can be found in most craft stores and sometimes in the paper and foil section of grocery stores. It's ideal for masking off areas of a stencil that you don't want to transfer, protecting work surfaces, and using, waxed side down, between the front and back of a T-shirt to keep paint from bleeding through the stencil onto the fabric. You can also make patterns from butcher paper.

Newspaper is also good for making patterns, and often you can get newspaper free, right out of the recycling bin. You can also buy large pads of unprinted newsprint at art supply stores. If you're using printed newspaper,

always test it first to make sure the ink does not rub off onto your fabric, and work gently with the newsprint since it tears easily.

Transparent **tracing paper** is ideal for developing textile designs or transferring stencils from a book or other object. It's lightweight and easy to see through for all of your tracing needs.

Tips on Making Paper Patterns

• Use a mechanical pencil when tracing or drawing garment patterns on paper. The pencil tip on these pencils always stays sharp and can be positioned closer to the ruler than a regular pencil, helping to ensure accuracy.

• When cutting out a pattern, aim the scissors just outside the pencil line because the paper always gives slightly and the scissors will end up cutting right along the line.

• To ensure smooth-edge cuts, never cut all the way to the scissors' tip; instead, cut halfway, then slide scissors up, and then cut again.

• When cutting patterns out of fabric, instead of pinning pattern to fabric, weight it down with paper weights (or with cans of tomatoes or anything heavy) and then trace around the pattern's edge with tailor's chalk.

Cutting Tools

Scissors

I'm very protective of my scissors and have my favorites for each task. My embroidery scissors are easily identified because I have a beat-up, old gray satin ribbon tied through one of the finger holes. "I think it's a tradition for all serious stitchers to be protective of their scissors," says patternmaker Jessica Bartlett. "Scissors are our most important tool, and it's true that a perfectly cut piece is crucial to the fit and look of the garment. Not just any scissor can accomplish that."

A good pair of **embroidery scissors** is essential for small, detailed work like intricate clipping and cutting thread. I've come to know and love classic 4" embroidery shears. For making longer cuts and trimming fabric, I prefer 5" knife-edge sewing and craft scissors.

For larger cutting projects like garments and patterns, **spring-loaded scissors** are a good, sturdy choice because the spring-loaded action helps prevent hand fatigue and makes it easier to cut clean, straight lines.

No sewing box is complete without a good pair of **paper scissors**. You'll use these for cutting out your paper garment patterns and for all sorts of other tasks that pop up as you proceed through your projects. Never, ever use your fabric scissors for cutting paper!

Seam Ripper

A seam ripper is a simple tool that helps you remove seams in sometimes hard-to-reach places. I use one mostly for taking pockets off T-shirts and for letting out hems. There are several styles of seam rippers available, so choose one that fits comfortably in your hand.

Rotary Cutter and Cutting Mat

A rotary cutter resembles a pizza cutter and has a round blade that cuts as you roll it along the fabric. It's helpful when cutting thin strips of fabric. Always use your rotary cutter with a cutting mat and a thick ruler to guide the blade and protect your fingers.

A cutting mat is a rubberlike pad that's essential when using a rotary cutter or craft knife, because it protects the work surface and helps stabilize the fabric as you cut. Cutting mats come with a plain or, more often, a gridded surface; the grid can help you cut straight and stay within the required measurements of your project.

Craft Knife

This knife has a razor-sharp blade that's ideal for cutting detailed shapes from paper, poster board, or stencil felt. Like a rotary cutter, this knife is best used with a cutting mat and must be handled very carefully to avoid injury. One of my design professors wisely advised that no one use craft knives or rotary cutters while working anywhere alone.

Tips on Scissor Care

If your scissors are getting dull, take them to a fabric store for sharpening. Also keep them clean (I clean mine with rubbing alcohol), so you don't get any unwanted stains on your projects. If your scissors start to "stick" when opening, use a cotton swab to apply a dab of WD-40 to the joint holding them together, then wipe down the scissors thoroughly to remove all of the WD-40 from the blades.

Pinning and Sewing Tools

Pins

My favorite pins are white-tipped quilting pins. Longer than average sewing pins, these have a large tip that my clumsy fingers can grab. Browse all the varieties of pins available, and find those that suit your fingers.

Needles

Like comfortable old T-shirts, needles tend to wear where they're loved most. Stitcher April Morgan says that all her needles become curved to the shape of her thumb because "I reckon I put so much pressure on them." So much pressure, in fact, that one day her favorite needle that her Grandma Bet had given her popped in half just like that. "I cried. I really did, because I thought I couldn't sew with any other needle."

Of course, April has since learned that she can sew with any needle; and, fortunately, needles come in a variety of shapes and sizes (see right). For most sewing, I like to use a sharp needle (in size #9), which is a medium-length hand-sewing needle with a round eye that's bigger than the average sewing needle and accommodates the thick buttonhole, carpet, and craft thread I regularly use. And since this needle is longer than many other needles, it helps me get my "sewing rhythm" because I can get more stitches on the needle as I move across the fabric.

Another way to keep your sewing groove is to thread several needles before starting work so that you don't have to stop and rethread your needle often. Stitcher Linda Williams will thread up to 25 needles at one time for a big project!

Needle Pullers and Thimbles

What I call needle pullers are rubber finger caps generally used by people who shuffle a lot of paper or cashiers who want to grab dollar bills easily. They are very helpful when you're trying to "get a grip" on your needle.

Thimbles can be extremely helpful as well, especially if you have delicate fingertips. It takes some time to get used to a thimble, but once you struggle through, you won't be able to sew without one. Thimbles come in many sizes and styles, and like a good pair of shoes, it's best to try them on before you take them home.

Needle-Nose Pliers

When sewing through many layers of fabric, it's sometimes necessary to have a pair of needle-nose pliers to pull the needle through. Don't be tempted to borrow one from the household tool kit because you don't want to get any dirt or oil residue from a household tool on your project. Instead, designate one pair of needle-nose pliers just for your sewing projects; label it so no one in the family will misuse it.

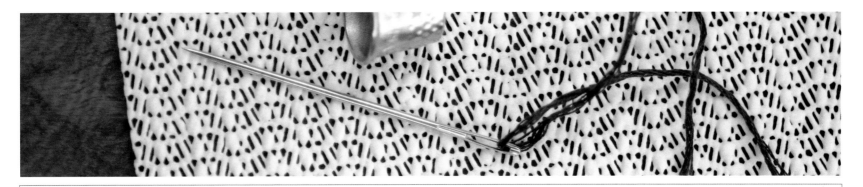

A Bird's-Eye Guide to Needles

Hand-sewing needles come in a variety of types and sizes. The sizes are based on the needle's length and thickness, which decrease as the number size increases. For example, a size #1 needle is thicker and longer than a size #12 needle. Here are a few of the types of needles readily available:

Ball point *(sizes 5-10)* This needle has a rounded tip and is used for many knit fabrics, but note that our experience has shown that ball points don't work well for tightly knit cotton-jersey fabric.

Beading *(sizes 10-15)* This type of needle is designed for sewing on beads and sequins but is difficult to use with the stronger buttonhole, carpet, and craft thread that we like because this thick thread does not pass easily through the needle's fine eye. For this reason, we often bead with a large-eye millinery needle (see right).

Between, or quilting *(sizes 1-12)* This needle is shorter than a standard needle and is designed to stitch through multiple layers of fabric.

Embroidery *(sizes 1-10)* This needle is like a sharp needle (see below) but has a longer eye that more easily accepts flosses and yarns for embroidery.

Leather, or glover's *(sizes 1-8)* This needle has a triangular point that pierces more easily through heavyweight fabrics like cotton duck and leather.

Millinery *(sizes 1-10)* Similar to a sharp needle (see below), a millinery needle is longer and hence especially well suited for basting, embroidery, and beadwork. Its eye is large enough to accommodate the heavy buttonhole, carpet, and craft thread we favor for sewing, so this is the needle that we choose most often for beading and other sewing projects.

Sharp *(sizes 1-12)* This is a basic, medium-length hand-sewing needle that's good for a wide variety of projects. This is the needle that we use for most of our projects. I have a preference for size #9.

Stenciling Tools

Clear Film

This transparent film is available at craft stores in the stencil-making section. I recommend that you use the medium- or heavy-weight film because thinner film makes the stencil-transfer process more difficult. This product is easier to cut than poster board and can be used with any stencil-transfer method (see right). Since this film is transparent, you can also trace any pattern directly on it with a permanent marker or use spray adhesive to affix a design printed on paper. While this film holds up well over time, be careful when storing it because it's very flexible; too much bending can damage your stencil.

Pennant Felt

Pennant felt is made from acrylic fibers and gets its name because it's often used for school pennants. I use it for making stencils. It's thin and sturdy and cuts easily with a craft knife, and the stencils made from it are flexible and durable. You can purchase this felt through specialty catalogs and online stores.

Spray Adhesive

Spray adhesive is a light glue released from a spray can and is available at hobby and craft shops. I use spray adhesive when making stencils and also when I transfer my patterns to fabric so that my stencil stays in place.

This helps me create a clean image with smooth edges that are easy to stitch around and embellish.

Stencil-Transfer Materials

Transferring stencils to fabric is one of the primary ways you'll embellish the projects in this book. Below are the materials that you can choose from to transfer your stencil pattern onto cotton jersey.

Sharpie markers are an easy but time-consuming tool for transferring patterns to fabric. They come in a variety of colors, and the marks they make last through many washings (except for the color red, which bleeds in the wash). To transfer a stencil with a Sharpie marker, trace around the cut-out areas of the design with the marker.

Textile paint is available at most craft stores and through many specialty catalogs. Some brands are packaged in spray cans, and others are packaged as liquid paint that you apply with a brush or airbrush gun. I use textile paints with an airbrush gun, which enables me to cover large areas quickly. You can purchase your own airbrush gun at a craft store or online for under $100. Another benefit of using an airbrush gun is that it allows you to regulate the amount of paint you're spraying so that you apply it evenly on your stencil.

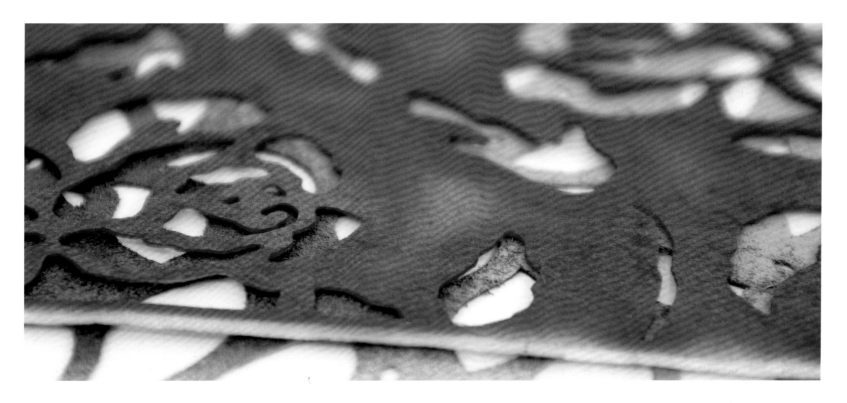

But don't feel like you have to buy an airbrush gun right away. Dabbing your textile paint on with a paint brush or sponge is an easy, effective way to color a stencil by hand. Applying paint by hand rather than with an airbrush gun also makes it easier for you to work neatly within the confines of the stencil without any over-spray. Note that many textile paints need to be heat-set according to the manufacturer's specifications in order to remain stable. Be sure to read and follow all instructions carefully, or your pattern could be gone with the first washing!

Cans of **spray enamel**, or standard spray paint, are available at hardware and many craft stores and are relatively inexpensive. These paints are easy to use; and, while not permanent, they do stay on your fabric for a long time. Additionally, no heat setting is necessary. The disadvantage of this paint is that it is damaging to the environment, has an extremely strong odor, and is difficult to remove from your hands after working. Be sure to read the label and carefully follow all of the manufacturer's instructions.

Beads and Beading Tools

Over time beads have been made from all types of materials—Native Americans used seeds, the Romans favored precious stones like pearls, and the Egyptians used glass. In the 1920s, flappers started a beading craze by adorning their dresses with the very first plastic beads, made from Bakelite. Today, beads come in a variety of materials, shapes, and sizes. As you become aware of all the types of beads available, you may enjoy collecting them as much as you do embellishing your projects with them. I use mainly bugle beads (elongated cylindrical beads) and seed beads (very small, rounded beads). These and many other varieties of beads can be found at local craft stores and in specialty catalogs.

Beading Needles and Thread

For beading, I like to use a #10 sharp needle or a large-eye millinery needle because the eye in these needles is big enough to accommodate the thick buttonhole, carpet, and craft thread I favor, but still small enough to pass through many beads (for beading, I use the thread as a single strand rather than doubled, as for regular sewing). However, some beads are even smaller than these needles, so always test to make sure that the beads you're considering can fit over your chosen needle.

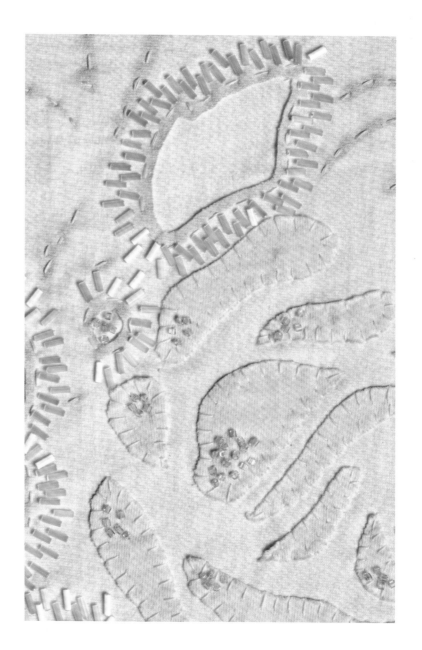

Types of Beading

Here are some of the types of beading that we use at Alabama Chanin (see also page 168 for information on beaded appliqué). You can work with any variety of beads and sequins for these methods.

Full beading (also called **armor beading**) fills in an area completely with beads.

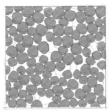  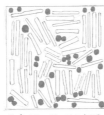

RANDOM SEED · RANDOM BUGLE · RANDOM MIXED

Half beading partially fills in an area with beads.

ORDERED SEED · ORDERED BUGLE · ORDERED MIXED

RANDOM SEED · RANDOM BUGLE · RANDOM MIXED

Outline beading simply outlines and embellishes any shape, print, or element.

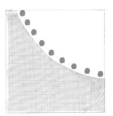 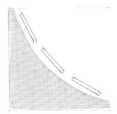

Fade beading begins as full beading, progresses to half beading, then finally disperses to nothing.

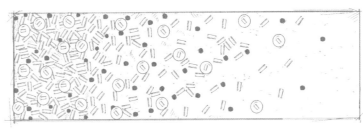

Seam beading adds a bugle bead or three seed beads to each stitch in a seam.

CHAPTER 3 | Stitches

I remember a sunny afternoon when I was about seven years old. My grandmother and I sat on her screened-in porch and stitched while she shared sewing tips and tales. The porch is still my favorite place to stitch, though on some evenings I curl up in my living room in my favorite red armchair printed with cream-colored roses. I hand-sew there using a small homemade, over-the-arm pincushion that I inherited from that same grandmother (see page 139 for the pattern). That little pincushion has seen a lot of use, but it still works perfectly. It keeps my tools close and makes me feel protected by my grandmother's presence.

Once you get started hand-stitching, you'll discover that it's much more than a creative outlet. Mary Anderson, who has worked in a car-parts factory for more than a decade, says that stitching puts her mind at ease and calms her nerves. My friend Shelby Wade likes to stitch under a shade tree, where she can relax and listen to the birds sing. I love to stitch when I have something weighing on my mind because it calms me and helps me think clearly.

In this chapter, you'll learn the basic hand stitches you need to get started on any of the projects in this book (all of them are sewn by hand), as well as some fancy hand stitches you can try once you get comfortable with a needle and thread. You'll find out the difference between basic stitches that don't stretch and stitches that do, and gather information to help you decide when to use these various stitches. Finally, you'll learn important knotting techniques and find out the best way to make a hand-stitched seam. The beauty of stitching is that everyone's stitches look a little different, so you can see a bit of yourself in every pull of the thread.

Learning to Stitch

My early sewing lessons were peppered with old wives' tales told by my mother, grandmother, and aunts. They taught me that thread should never be longer than the distance from your fingers to your elbow and that when you stick your finger and bleed on your work, the only way to get that blood out is with your own spit.

I've come to learn that in every old wives' tale there is a smidgen of truth: There are disadvantages to having your thread too long (and a bit of saliva *will*, in fact, dissolve blood on fabric). A long thread will tangle and knot more easily, and you might spend more time pulling the thread than actually sewing. Fellow stitcher Jo Ann Stokes is notorious for her very long threads. She likes it that way, but anyone in her vicinity has to be careful not to sit on her "pulling side" because she might just poke you with her needle when she pulls that long thread.

You might already know that you love sewing with a long thread or a shorter one, but if you don't, your likes and dislikes as well as your strengths and weaknesses will become very clear as you continue to stitch. Following are a few tips to think about as you begin.

Chalking Your Stitching Line

When I first started stitching, I found it necessary to use tailor's chalk (see page 22) to trace out my stitching line in order to sew at a consistently even distance from the fabric's cut edge. Chalking your stitching line is a great technique that quickly teaches you how to gauge your seam allowance and stitch a perfectly straight line.

To chalk your stitching line, simply mark your seams with a line 1/4" from the fabric's edge using tailor's chalk and a small ruler (see below).

Chalking Your Stitching Line

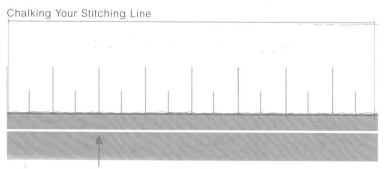

USE RULER TO CHALK LINE 1/4" FROM EDGE.

Finding Your Stitching Rhythm

In the beginning when you start sewing, you might find yourself "stab-stitching," or pulling every individual stitch through, first to one side of the fabric and then to the other side. This technique is helpful when you're sewing through many layers of fabric that are difficult for the needle to pass through, but it's not necessary all the time and can slow down your stitching a lot.

At a recent sewing circle with some friends, I pointed out to Trey Williams that he was stab-stitching every time he sewed a stitch. I showed him that you can do what's called a running stitch by weaving the needle in and out of the fabric several times, collecting the stitches in a row on the needle before pulling the thread through (you'll find more about this stitch on page 36). After he got the hang of it and was moving along at a nice pace, he asked me, "What do you call that now?" "Sewing," I answered, "I think that you call that sewing."

The Importance of Stitch Length

At Alabama Chanin, we have developed our own guidelines for stitch length. Stitches that are too long can snag and break (if you can insert a standard number 2 pencil through any of your stitches, they're too long). Stitches that are too short can pull right through the fabric and create unwanted holes. As a rule, when working on the projects in this book, your stitches should be no longer than $\frac{1}{4}$" and no shorter than $\frac{1}{8}$". Pay close attention to both the wrong side and the right side of your project, and aim for uniform stitches that look the same on both sides of the fabric.

Tension in Hand-Sewing

In hand-sewing, the tension of your stitching determines how tight or loose the stitches are. If your tension is too tight—that is, if you pull your thread too tight as you sew through the fabric—your seam will be pulled too tight and will gather. If your tension is too loose, your seam will be sewn too loosely and will buckle.

You can control tension by using your fingers to guide the stitches. After completing each pull of your needle, check your tension to make sure that your fabric lies flat, smooth, and even. Adjust the tension of the stitches you've sewn by holding onto both sides of your project and giving a gentle pull to make the fabric lie perfectly flat. You can also place your thumb on the bottom of your project fabric and your index finger on the top and gently rub that thread in the direction of your stitches to get the perfect tension. Once you get into a stitching rhythm, this manipulation will become second nature.

The Stitches

What I call stitching is really a combination of quilting and embroidery. I've divided the stitches presented here into two groups—those that don't stretch and those that do—since these two types of stitches are applied in different areas on our projects.

Basic Stitches That Don't Stretch

Although these basic stitches may seem mundane and lacking decorative flair, each of them has an important function. So take the time to learn these three stitches—the straight (or running) stitch, backstitch, and basting stitch—because they'll carry you through the projects in this book and beyond. Note that in some of the stitch directions, you'll be instructed to pull the thread up from the back of the fabric to start the stitch. But you could just as easily start the stitch from the front of the fabric, which would mean that the knot and thread tails would be visible on the right side of the project. We like to do this, and you'll find that the project directions, therefore, oftentimes tell you to start stitching on the right side of the fabric. In either case, the difference is simply whether the knot is hidden on the garment's wrong side or visible on its right side. (For related information on the heavyweight thread I recommend stitching with for these and the stretchable stitches that follow, see page 20, where you will also find information on why thread knots and how to keep thread from tangling when you stitch.)

The **straight (or running) stitch** is the most basic stitch of all and is used in this book for both general construction and for embellishing a fabric with reverse appliqué and beading. Its two names refer to the way it "runs" in a "straight" line. This is the stitch that my grandmothers and aunts used to make all of their quilts. Always follow the guidelines for stitch length on page 35 when using this stitch on cotton jersey.

Straight (or Running) Stitch

BRING NEEDLE FROM BACK OF FABRIC AT A, GO BACK DOWN AT B, AND COME OUT AT C, MAKING STITCHES AND SPACES BETWEEN THEM THE SAME LENGTH.

To make this stitch, work from right to left, as shown above, and make both your stitches and the spaces between them between $\frac{1}{8}$" and $\frac{1}{4}$" in length. Your stitching should look the same on the front and back of the fabric.

Backstitch

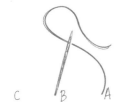 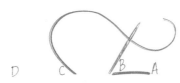 

BRING NEEDLE UP AT A, GO BACK DOWN AT B, AND EXIT AT C. THEN STITCH BACK IN JUST AHEAD OF B, COME UP AT D, STITCH BACK IN JUST AHEAD OF C, AND COME UP AT E, CONTINUING THIS OVERALL PATTERN.

The **backstitch** is really just another form of straight stitch that fills in the entire stitching line with thread and looks very much like a machine stitch. It may seem confusing at first to work "backwards" with this stitch to move forward, but the backstitch is very easy to learn. A durable stitch for any project, the backstitch is especially good for outlining a shape or an area of your work. To sew the backstitch, see the illustration above.

A **basting stitch** is a long, temporary stitch that's really just a looser, longer version of the straight stitch, which is used to hold, or baste, layers of fabric together as you

Basting Stitch

MAKE BOTH STITCHES AND SPACES BETWEEN THEM ABOUT ½" LONG.

construct or embellish your project. A basting stitch also helps preserve the shape of the cut fabric and prevent a cut edge, like a curved neckline, from stretching as you work. Machine sewers routinely stay-stitch—that is, machine-sew using a regular-length stitch near a cut edge to stabilize it and prevent it from stretching; when sewing by hand, basting stitches of about ½" in length serve the same purpose.

To baste, use a single (rather than doubled) strand of all-purpose thread to sew simple basting stitches on any layers you want to hold in place during construction and on all your necklines and armholes to keep them from stretching. There's no need to knot the thread at the beginning or end of a line of basting stitches since you want to be able to remove these stitches easily later. As with a straight stitch, keep the length of your stitches consistent, and make the spaces between stitches about the same length as the stitches themselves, about ½" long (see the illustration at left).

Basic Stitches That Stretch

I learned the hard way why it's important to use stretchable stitches around necklines, armholes, and other places where you need some stretch. In the beginning, I used a regular straight stitch around a T-shirt neckline but then couldn't get the neck over my head because the stitches wouldn't allow the fabric to "give." I realized very quickly that, because stretchable stitches involve inserting and pulling the needle and thread out of the fabric at angles, they allow the cotton jersey to maintain its natural ability to stretch. All of the stitches that follow can be used for areas that require stretch. As an added plus, each of these stretchable stitches is also decorative. Always test your stretchable stitch to make sure that it really does have enough stretch for your project. You can add to a seam's stretchability by simply increasing the length of your stitches.

The **zigzag chain stitch** is a good stitch to use in areas requiring a lot of stretch. A zigzag chain stitch is worked right to left on the fabric, as shown below.

Zigzag Chain Stitch

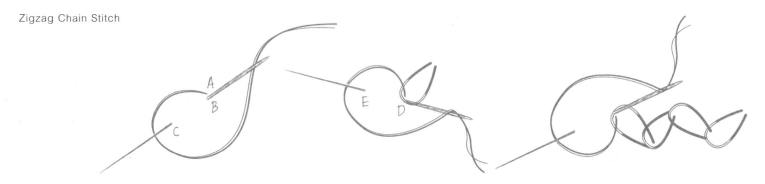

COME UP AT A AND FORM THREAD LOOP, GO BACK DOWN AT B (VERY CLOSE TO A BUT NOT IN IT), AND COME BACK UP AT C, PLACING NEEDLE TIP OVER THREAD, AND PULL THREAD THROUGH. FORM ANOTHER LOOP AND INSERT NEEDLE AT D INTO THREAD OF FIRST LOOP TO KEEP IT IN PLACE, BRING NEEDLE OUT AT E, PLACING NEEDLE TIP OVER THREAD, AND PULL THREAD THROUGH. CONTINUE TO WORK THESE BASIC STEPS, ALTERNATING FROM SIDE TO SIDE, TO FORM ZIGZAG CHAIN.

The **cross-stitch** has lots of stretch, is easy to learn, and is excellent for beginning stitchers. Work a cross-stitch left to right, as shown below.

Cross-Stitch

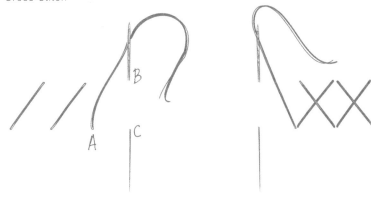

COME UP AT A, BACK DOWN AT B, AND UP AGAIN AT C TO MAKE SLANTED STITCH. CONTINUE THIS TO END OF ROW. THEN WORK SAME STITCH IN OPPOSITE DIRECTION FROM LOWER RIGHT TO UPPER LEFT, OVER PREVIOUS STITCHES, TO FORM X.

The **parallel whipstitch** is the most basic of the stretchable embroidery stitches. I like to use this stitch to decoratively attach appliqué (see page 63) or any other decorative element on a garment. Work this stitch, as shown below, making the stitches and the spaces between them both $3/8$". (This stitch can also be used to wrap an edge to finish it, as, for example, in the Sampler Quilt on page 171. In this case, in the drawing below, you would bring your needle up at A, wrap the thread over the edge, and come back up $3/8$" to the right of A to begin the next stitch, continuing this pattern the full length of the edge being finished.)

Parallel Whipstitch

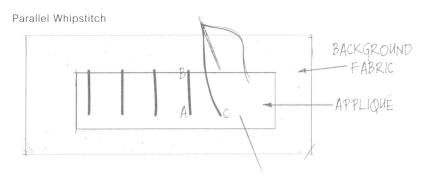

COME UP AT A, GO BACK DOWN AT B, AND COME UP AGAIN AT C. REPEAT THIS PATTERN TO WHIPSTITCH APPLIQUE TO BACKGROUND FABRIC.

The Importance of Knotting Off Properly

Knots are the anchor for all stitching; and when I started hand-sewing cotton-jersey garments, I placed all my knots on the right side for the world to see. It first occurred to me to do this on a Saturday afternoon at the 26th Street Flea Market in New York City. There, I found a beautiful turn-of-the-century corset that had seen lots of wear and repair. I was so struck by the intricate handwork on the inside of this garment that, in that moment, I decided that I didn't want to hide anything.

Showing off the beauty of structure has become a foundation of my work. But as my collections have evolved over the years, I've found that I want to be flexible. So today, I decide design by design whether to show all my knots, hide them, or combine the two approaches in one piece. But hidden or seen, knots always serve the extremely important technical purpose of keeping hand-sewn projects sturdy and durable.

Especially in hand-sewing, your knot holds your entire seam. If you lose that knot, you will lose the seam. And since cotton-jersey fabric is a knit made up of a series of tiny thread loops, if you use a small knot, that knot can pull through these small loops and may even break one or more of them, causing the fabric to "run" and produce an even bigger hole. That's why the project directions in this book will usually tell you to double your thread and use large double knots (see below).

Another way to ensure durability with knots is to leave a long tail of about a $\frac{1}{2}$" of thread after you tie off each knot. Wearing and washing your garment over time will cause these thread tails to become shorter and shorter, and can wear up to $\frac{1}{4}$" off the thread tails. For this reason, if you start with long tails, you can ensure that the garment maintains its original integrity from the first day it was knotted. I laughingly say I like to leave the long tails for future generations.

Tying a Double Knot

It's important to tie your knots in a particular way to make them neat and durable. Once you've threaded your needle, tie off a double strand with a double knot as shown at right. When you've finished a section and need to cut your thread, make a loop with your needle and then pull the needle through the loop, using your forefinger or thumb to nudge the knot into place, so it's flush with the fabric. Then repeat this process a second time to make a double knot. When you cut your thread, leave a $\frac{1}{2}$" tail after the second knot. You'll find that separating the threads and tying the knot (like tying your shoelace) produces a knot that unravels easily and whose tails splay out to the sides.

Tying a Double Knot

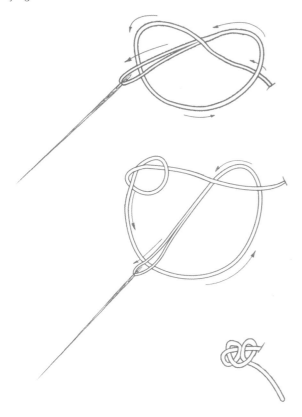

MAKE LOOP WITH THREAD, BRING NEEDLE UP THROUGH
LOOP AS SHOWN, TO CREATE KNOT, AND PULL THREAD
TO TIGHTEN KNOT CLOSE TO FABRIC. MAKE SECOND
LOOP, AND BRING NEEDLE UP THROUGH LOOP, AS
BEFORE, TO CREATE SECOND KNOT, CAREFULLY PULLING
THREAD TO TIGHTEN KNOT DIRECTLY OVER FIRST
KNOT TO CREATE DOUBLE KNOT.

Knots as Design Elements

After "loving" the thread (see page 21) and tying it off
with a double knot (see left), we often start stitching from
the right side of a piece so that the knot will be visible
and become part of the stitched pattern on the piece. In
the case of appliqué or reverse appliqué embellishment
(see pages 62 and 64), which call for stitching around each
shape in a stencil design, the knots themselves become
design elements. See the examples below of knotting off
on the right side (top) and wrong side (bottom).

Seams

When I look at buckskin garments that were worn by Native Americans and some American frontiersmen, I'm struck by the beauty, strength, and durability of their hand-sewn seams, which were often enhanced with beads and special knots. I pride myself on my own strong, hand-stitched seams and regard them as yet another way to show off my handwork. Because I use a strong, heavyweight thread (see page 20), my seams tend to be stronger than machine-stitched seams, and I incorporate that seam strength into my designs.

Each season I ask a basic question about seams: Do I want to see all of that handwork on the right side of my designs, or do I prefer to have a more streamlined look and keep the seams and seam allowances hidden on the wrong side? As a general rule, all of my seams are $\frac{1}{4}$" wide (that is, I stitch the seam line $\frac{1}{4}$" from the fabric's cut raw edge, and I use two types of seams, which I call floating seams and felled seams.

Floating Seams

This seam's name refers to the fact that, after the seam is stitched, the seam allowances are left untouched, or "floating," that is, not stitched down (see right). When you use floating seams in a project, it's important to do so consistently and to make sure that every seam "floats,"

even seams that intersect. To stitch a floating seam that intersects another floating seam, stitch under the sewn seam being intersected so that its allowances remain floating, and then begin stitching again as usual on the seam you're sewing (see below). You can sew a floating seam on the right side or the wrong side of a project.

Floating Seam

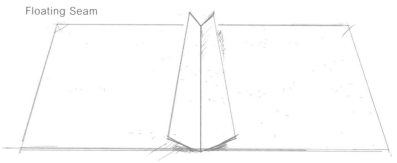

STITCH SEAM, BUT LEAVE SEAM ALLOWANCES FLOATING (NOT STITCHED DOWN).

WHEN STITCHING INTERSECTING FLOATING SEAMS, SEW UNDER INTERSECTING SEAM, SO ITS ALLOWANCES REMAIN FLOATING.

A **floating seam on the right side** of a project is made by pinning the two cut fabrics being seamed with their wrong sides together and then stitching the seam on the right side of the fabric. The seam allowances of the resulting seam are visible on the right side, or outside, of the project (see below).

A **floating seam on the wrong side** of a project is made by pinning the two cut fabrics being seamed with their right sides together, and then stitching the seam on the wrong side of the fabric. The seam allowances of the resulting seam are visible on the wrong side, or inside, of the project (see below).

Floating Seam on Right Side

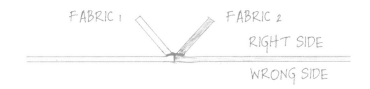

Floating Seam on Wrong Side

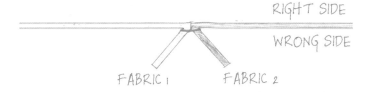

Seeing Your Stitches

When hand-sewing, it's very important to have good lighting. If you don't have strong light from above, you won't be able to see detail, and your eyes will get strained and tire quickly. Our stitchers swear by the "daylight" lamps sold at many craft stores. A great trick to help bring your work closer to your sight range is to put a pillow on your lap and stitch with your project on top of it. That way, you have a steady surface to work on and a place into which to stick spare needles and pins. Some of our stitchers like to use the U-shaped nursing pillows that fit up around your waist. This type of pillow stays steady and also supports your elbows.

Felled Seams

My felled seam is a variation on the traditional flat-felled seam sewn on a sewing machine that hides all of the seam allowances' cut edges. On my felled seam, the cut edges of the seam allowances still show, but, unlike on a floating seam, these allowances are sewn down with a row of stitches parallel to the seam line.

Sewing my felled seam is easy: First, you work a regular floating seam, then you fold that seam's seam allowances over to one side and stitch them down flat to the garment with a second row of stitches parallel to the seam line (see top right). A felled seam can be sewn on the right side or the wrong side of a project.

To sew a **felled seam on the right side** of a project, start by sewing a floating seam on the right side (see bottom right). Then fold the finished seam's allowances over to one side, and stitch them down with a row of parallel stitches $\frac{1}{8}$" from the allowances cut edges (or you could stitch at $\frac{1}{4}$" from the cut edges, which would be down the center of the seam allowances). The resulting seam is visible on the right side of the project.

Felled Seam

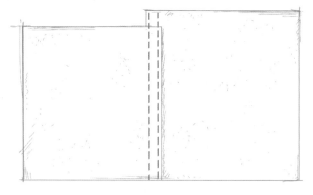

Felled Seam on Right Side

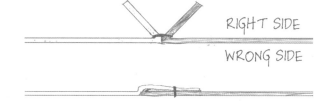

RIGHT SIDE

WRONG SIDE

To sew a **felled seam on the wrong side** of a project, start by sewing a floating seam on the wrong side. Then fold the finished seam's allowances over to one side, and stitch them down on the wrong side of the project with a row of parallel stitches $\frac{1}{8}$" from the allowances' cut edges (or you could stitch at $\frac{1}{8}$" from the cut edges, which would be down the center of the seam allowances). The resulting seam is invisible on the right side of the project (see below).

Felled Seam on Wrong Side

Wrap-Stitching Your Seams

You should wrap-stitch all your seams, that is, begin and end each seam by wrapping the first and last stitches around the raw edges of the fabric. Do this by wrapping a loop of thread around the edge of the fabric to anchor your seam, as shown in the illustration below. Stitching a seam without this wrap-stitch can allow your fabric to slide up or down the seam, causing it to gather and pull.

Wrap-Stitching Your Seams

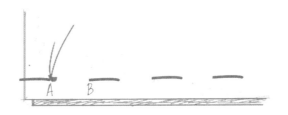

MAKE A DOUBLE KNOT (SEE PAGE 40), AND INSERT NEEDLE AT A, WRAP THREAD AROUND SIDE OF FABRIC TO FRONT, AND GO BACK IN AT A, THEN COME UP AT B, AND START STITCHING SEAM.

Which Direction to Fell Your Seams?

When deciding which direction to fell your seams on a garment, start at the center front or center back and always fell seams toward the side of your body. As a general rule, side seams should be felled towards the back.

CHAPTER 4 | Techniques

Most of the techniques you will learn in this chapter are nothing new. Many are based on the quilting and embroidery techniques of the Depression-era South, and others have been practiced by artisans for hundreds of years. I have borrowed this knowledge and made it the foundation of most of my designs. In this chapter, I pass this knowledge on to you, hoping that you'll use it to make beautiful, soulful, rich, and strong clothing and textiles.

First you'll find instructions on how to dissect, or deconstruct, a cotton-jersey T-shirt, which provides you with the fabric for each of the projects in this book. From there, you'll learn the best way to handle and cut cotton jersey. Finally, you'll get the basic techniques for embellishing projects with stencils, appliqué, reverse appliqué, and beading.

Deconstructing a T-Shirt

I've been working with recycled T-shirts for years, and they're the basis for all of our designs. In any given season, I have deconstructed thousands of T-shirts to produce a collection. I've probably seen every brand of T-shirt that has ever existed and in every shape, size, color, and quality produced.

Finding the Grain Line

The first step in deconstructing a T-shirt is finding its grain line. The term *grain line* refers to the weave or knit of a fabric, and, in the case of a knitted cotton-jersey T-shirt, the grain line usually runs vertically from the top of the shirt to the bottom. The grain line is visible on the fabric's right side, or face, which is generally used as the right side of the T-shirt. If you look closely at cotton jersey's right side, you'll see straight vertical columns of stitches that make up the grain line, as shown at right.

On cotton jersey's wrong side (which is most often used as the T-shirt's wrong side), you won't see the vertical columns of the grain line. Instead, on the wrong side, you'll see a series of little loops (see right).

Although, in most T-shirts, the grain line runs from the top of the collar down to the bottom of the shirt, so the fabric stretches across the body, some fashion T-shirts may not

Cotton Jersey's Right Side

Cotton Jersey's Wrong Side

follow this custom. Instead, they may be constructed so that the grain line runs horizontally around the body or maybe in different directions in various parts of the shirt. For this reason, always identify the grain line of your T-shirt fabric before you start cutting out your project. And, when you're ready to cut out the project, make sure that the fabric's grain line and the grain line marked on your pattern run in the same direction.

If you're unsure about finding the grain line, gently pull the fabric to stretch it and make the grain line easier to see. Note that when the fabric is cut *with* the grain line (that is, in the same direction as the grain line), the cut edges will roll to the fabric's wrong side. Conversely, when the fabric is cut across or *against* the grain, the cut edges will curl to the fabric's right side.

Directions for Deconstruction

Supplies
Cotton-jersey T-shirt

Seam ripper

Garment scissors

1. Remove Pocket
If the T-shirt has a pocket, remove it with a seam ripper. Work slowly and carefully to rip out the stitches attaching the pocket; it's very easy to make a hole in the T-shirt itself while removing the corners.

Sometimes after removing a pocket, you'll find a ghost image where the pocket was sewn, protecting the T-shirt fabric underneath from fading. We love these kinds of shadow images and always incorporate them into our designs.

2. Detach Neckline Ribbing
Inspect the neckline ribbing to find out if and where it was sewn together with a seam. Some ribbing is manufactured on a circular knitting machine to fit the neckline perfectly without a seam. If your ribbing has a seam, use your garment scissors to make your first cut down the middle of that seam. If your ribbing doesn't have a seam, make your first cut through the ribbing at the shoulder seam. Cut through all layers and all the way through the seam that joins the neckline ribbing to the body of the shirt. Then turn your scissors, and cut just beyond the seam line attaching the ribbing to the T-shirt body to remove as much of the ribbing as possible (see bottom left). We generally save this neckline ribbing to incorporate into other projects.

3. Detach Sleeves
Using garment scissors, detach the sleeves from the body of the T-shirt. Cut through each sleeve along the seam line joining it to the body (cutting on the sleeve side rather than body) and along the underarm seam (see bottom right).

Detach Neckline Ribbing *(Step 2)*

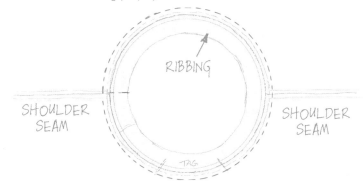

CUT ALONG RED DASHED LINE.

Detach Sleeves *(Step 3)*

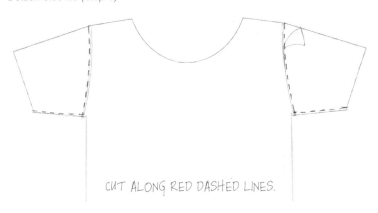

CUT ALONG RED DASHED LINES.

4. Separate Shoulder Seams

Separate the front of the T-shirt from the back at the shoulders by cutting along the shoulder seams (see right).

You'll end up with a tube of fabric that looks like the illustrations at right on the facing page.

The tube can then be cut in one of three ways to make the

Separate Shoulder Seams *(Step 4)*

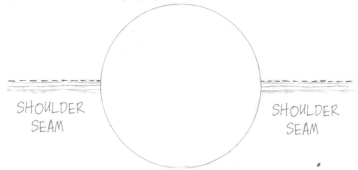

CUT ALONG RED DASHED LINES.

Picking a T-Shirt

When selecting a T-shirt to work with, don't be put off by a shirt with a stain or a printed graphic. Simply cut the pattern from the part of the T-shirt that's unstained or unprinted. If your project calls for a stenciled design, you can superimpose the stencil over the stain; and cut the stain away when you cut out the interior shapes of the design. If you're working with a T-shirt with a printed graphic, you may even want to incorporate the graphic into your design, as we did with the Printed T-Shirt Corset on page 155.

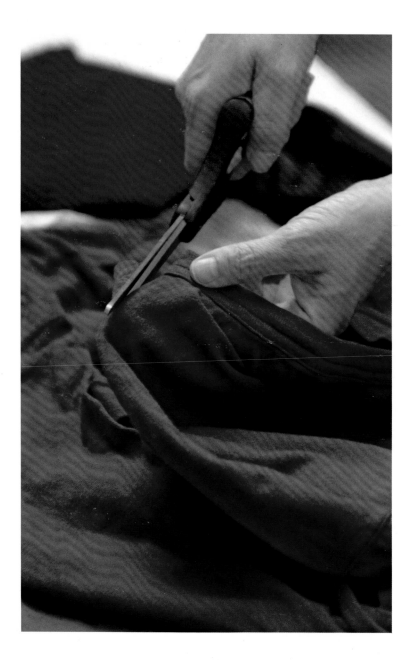

fabric for your project, and the project directions will always tell you which way to cut the tube: It can be cut up the center front, so it can open out and lie flat; it can be cut from the bottom edge below one armhole up to the center of that armhole, so, again, the tube can open out and lie flat; or it can be cut on both sides from the bottom edge up to the center-armhole to create two separate fabric panels.

Some T-shirts are made with side seams; others are manufactured on circular knitting machines, which produce a seamless tube. If your T-shirt has side seams, you'll probably want to cut the T-shirt tube into separate front and back panels. If your T-shirt is seamless, you can cut it in any of the three ways.

Deconstructed T-Shirt

Tube of Fabric

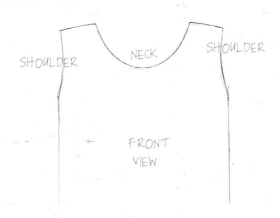

SHOULDER NECK SHOULDER

FRONT VIEW

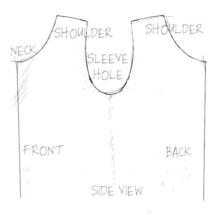

NECK SHOULDER SHOULDER
SLEEVE HOLE
FRONT BACK
SIDE VIEW

Other Deconstructed Parts

SLEEVES REMOVED AND SPLIT OPEN

POCKET

RIBBING

Cutting Out Patterns

Whether you work with ready-made patterns or make your own patterns, cutting out a pattern requires precision. For some of the projects in this book, we've provided ready-made patterns; for the others, we've given you instructions on how to create the patterns yourself.

Guidelines for Cutting Patterns

Supplies
Deconstructed cotton-jersey T-shirt or cotton-jersey fabric

Project pattern

Tailor's chalk

Paper scissors

Garment scissors

1. Choose Size and Cut Out Paper Pattern
The garment patterns at the back of this book include five sizes (from XS to XL) in which the garment can be made. Decide which size you want to make (see right), photocopy the pattern, and use your paper scissors to cut out the photocopied pattern in your desired size.

2. Prepare Fabric for Cutting and Stitching
Before cutting your cotton jersey, you'll need to decide if you're going to cut it folded double-layer or laid flat as a single layer (see page 54).

Whichever way you choose, prevent the cotton jersey from stretching as you work by patting it lightly into place with your fingertips on your work surface. Do not pull on or stretch the cotton jersey with your fingers.

3. Transfer Pattern to Fabric
Lay all of your paper pattern pieces on top of your fabric, making sure the pattern's marked grain line runs in the same direction as the fabric's grain line (see page 48) to ensure that you're cutting out the pattern piece correctly. This is important because, for example, when cutting out a corset, you want the grain line on the cut fabric pieces to run vertically from the neckline to the bottom of the corset in order to ensure that the fabric stretches around your body.

As you trace around your pattern piece with tailor's chalk, hold the pattern in place with the palm of your hand (or with pattern weights or even canned goods). We prefer holding or weighting the pattern to pinning it on the fabric, which, in the case of cotton jersey, often skews the fabric and makes the cutting uneven. This strategy also prevents the nicks and tears in the pattern that pinning often causes.

4. Cut Pattern from Fabric
Using garment scissors, cut out the pattern pieces, trying your best to cut just inside the chalked line you traced around the pattern. By cutting away all the visible chalk (but not cutting beyond the chalked line), you'll help ensure a perfect fit.

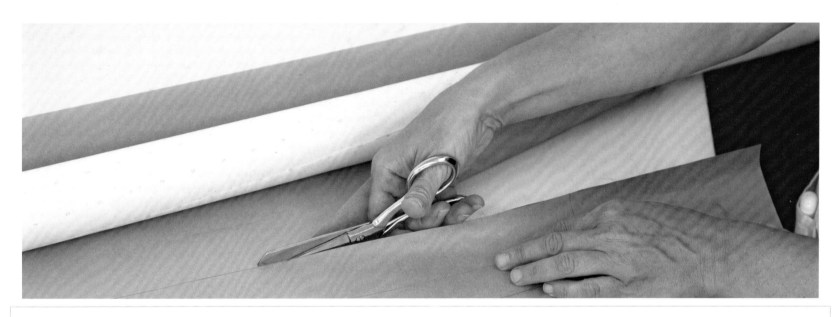

Finding Your Size

When it comes to picking a size, everyone has a personal preference. Over the years, I've found that I'm happiest with my garments when the fit is slightly snug. If you, too, like a snug fit, I recommend cutting your pattern one size smaller than you'd usually wear since T-shirt jersey stretches easily. As you wear the garment, the cotton knit will "relax" and begin to take on the shape of your body. The only exception to this guideline would be if you're making a project that's heavily embellished with decorative stitching and beading since the embellishment tends to limit the cotton jersey's ability to stretch. In that case, I recommend using a pattern one size larger than usual. But whatever your fit preference, to help you choose a pattern size to produce the fit you like, reference the general size chart below.

	XS	S	M	L	XL
Size	0	0-2	4-6	8-10	12-14
Chest	28-31	32-35	36-39	40-43	44-46
Waist	23-24	25-26	27-29	30-32	33-35

Fabric—Cut It Single- or Double-Layer?

When cutting out a pattern, you'll work either with the fabric opened out flat as a single layer or with it folded double-layer (the directions for each project in this book will tell you which way to work with the fabric). If the directions call for cutting the pattern with the fabric laid flat as a single layer, the pieces you cut will exactly duplicate the pattern's shape (see below). Cutting pattern pieces on a single layer of flat fabric enables you to use up fabric scraps, such as the sleeves taken off the T-shirt when you deconstructed it or remnants left after you cut other pattern pieces.

If the directions call for cutting a pattern piece "on the fold," that means to fold the fabric in half (double-layer) lengthwise along its grain line (see page 48) and to align the edge of the pattern piece marked "Place on fold" on the fold of the fabric (see top right). The pattern for the front or back of a garment or for a sleeve is often cut on the fold. When unfolded, the cut piece will double the shape of the pattern piece, with the side unfolded a mirror image of the pattern's shape.

Some projects call for cutting with the fabric double-layer but not on the fold. This means that you'll place the pattern piece on the folded fabric away from the fold, and cutting around the pattern piece will produce two fabric duplicates of the pattern piece, with one of them a mirror image (see bottom right). You could also layer two different fabrics laid flat as single layers, with both right side up, to make up the double layer if you wanted two exact duplicate pieces cut in fabrics of different colors.

There is one special instance of cutting patterns on two single layers of fabric laid flat: when you're cutting two different colors of fabric for reverse appliqué. Because we've found it works best to have the backing fabric for reverse appliqué just slightly larger all around—by about $1/16$"—than the top fabric, here's how we cut these pieces: First, we trace the paper pattern pieces right side up on the top fabric, and cut them out. Then we place the cut fabric pieces (not the paper pattern pieces) on the right side of the backing fabric, and carefully cut very close around, but not into, each cut fabric "pattern." Using the cut fabric pieces as patterns instead of the paper pattern automatically gives an extra $1/16$" on the pieces cut from the backing fabric.

Cutting on Single-Layer Fabric

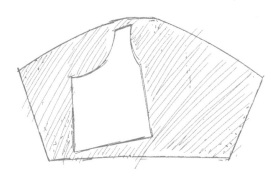

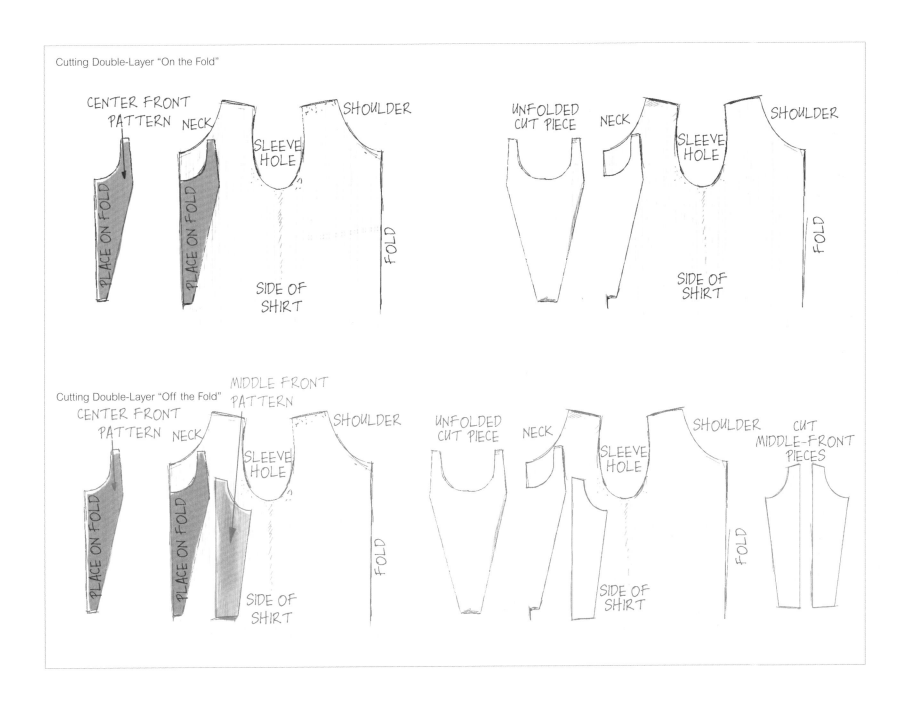

Cutting Double-Layer "On the Fold"

CENTER FRONT PATTERN

PLACE ON FOLD

PLACE ON FOLD

NECK

SLEEVE HOLE

SHOULDER

SIDE OF SHIRT

FOLD

UNFOLDED CUT PIECE

NECK

SLEEVE HOLE

SHOULDER

SIDE OF SHIRT

FOLD

Cutting Double-Layer "Off the Fold"

CENTER FRONT PATTERN

MIDDLE FRONT PATTERN

PLACE ON FOLD

PLACE ON FOLD

NECK

SLEEVE HOLE

SHOULDER

SIDE OF SHIRT

FOLD

UNFOLDED CUT PIECE

NECK

SLEEVE HOLE

SHOULDER

SIDE OF SHIRT

FOLD

CUT MIDDLE-FRONT PIECES

Stenciling

Stenciling has a long history in America and around the globe. The Colonists stenciled decorations like flowers, fruits, and hearts on their furniture, walls, and floorboards to brighten up their dark, sometimes bleak farmhouses. During the Victorian era, elaborate stencils were used to adorn ceilings and walls with ornate patterns. At Alabama Chanin, we use stencils to transfer decorative designs to fabric all the time.

Every season I develop a variety of stencils that often reflect my inspiration for that collection. Once I was inspired by the naturalism of nineteenth-century English painter Dante Gabriel Rossetti as well as the romance of the late country singer Patsy Cline, who had a penchant for elaborate costumes. I wanted to design a collection combining many influences, so I made gowns embellished with roses, ruffles, and beads, all with a country-and-western twist.

When I started making T-shirts in New York, the first stencils I ever used were block numbers made out of brown kraft paper—the kind of numbers sold at hardware stores to spray-paint addresses on curbs. When I came back to Alabama, I began experimenting more. In the beginning, there were simple stencils like the Rooster on page 88. Then we progressed to more elaborate designs like the Rose on page 113. After you begin making stencils, you'll realize that you can find patterns practically everywhere. I once took a glass fixture off the ceiling, traced a climbing rose pattern from it, and turned the pattern into a stencil. But most of the time, it's much easier. In fact, there are plenty of books filled with ready-to-use stencils. I love to look through these books and, even with all of my experience, I often find designs in them that I want to incorporate into my collections.

If you are new to stenciling, you might want to use the pullout stencil provided with this book (after page 144) or the ready-made stencils available in many craft and art supply stores. Or use the following directions to make your own stencils.

Tips for Making and Using Stencils

• In the beginning, make your stencils with poster board. It's easy to cut; and, if you make a mistake, it's not costly to replace. Once you get the hang of making stencils and create ones you want to use over and over again, you might be happier to cut your stencils out of pennant felt (see page 28).

• Take proper care of your stencils, and you'll be able to use them again and again. Always dry them thoroughly before storing, and store them where they can lie flat and undisturbed.

• Always double-check to see that you've traced around or filled in all of your stencil shapes before picking up a stencil since it's difficult to reposition the stencil exactly as it was once you've moved it.

• If you're using paint to transfer your stencil, test your color on a piece of scrap fabric before starting to paint the stencil on your project. Paint tends to dry lighter, and you want to make sure that you like your color (in reverse appliqué, you'll have a sliver of that color left after trimming the interior of each shape; see page 65) and that you can see it well enough to stitch around it.

• Remember that a stencil is just a guide. If you don't like part of the stencil, cover it up with masking tape (or with butcher paper and tape for large areas) or don't trace or transfer that part. You may also find that you want to trace additional single elements of a stencil like single leaves or small leaf clusters to fill in areas, which is fine. The way you use your stencil is limited only by your imagination.

Making a Stencil

Supplies

Stencil design

Poster board *(slightly larger than desired size of stencil)*

Spray adhesive

Craft knife with sharp blade

Computer with scanning capabilities *(optional)*

1. Choose and Scan or Photocopy Stencil Design

A stencil design is really just a silhouetted image or piece of art that's transferred to the surface being stenciled, whether that surface is fabric, wood, paper, glass, or another material. To create a stencil design, you need an image and a method for transferring the image to the surface you want to decorate.

The first step is to photocopy your image if it's printed; or, if it's on a CD or scanned into your computer, to enlarge or reduce the image to the size you want, and then print it out. If you want the image to be larger than the letter-sized paper used by most home printers and copiers, take it to a copy shop that can scale it to the size you want and print it out.

2. Affix Stencil Design to Poster Board

Working in a well-ventilated area and following the instructions on the spray adhesive's label, spray the back of the paper printout of your stencil design with a light coating of spray adhesive. Then affix the paper to a piece of poster board. The spray adhesive will keep the image from shifting, and the poster board will make the stencil sturdy.

3. Cut Out Stencil Design

Place the poster board with your design face up on a cutting mat. Use the tip of the craft knife to cut out all the black or colored areas and create a stencil that's a negative image of your original piece of art (see below).

Note that it's important that your craft knife has a sharp blade in order to get a precise cut. Also, be sure to cut carefully and slowly to avoid injury.

4. Test Stencil

It's always a good idea to test your stencil before transferring it to your project fabric. To do this, lay it on top of a piece of paper or poster board, and use your favorite method for stencil transfer (see page 28) to fill entirely all the areas that you cut out. The resulting image from your stencil shows you exactly how it will look on your fabric. As an added benefit of testing, you've also created a back-up image that can be cut into a new stencil if the original gets lost or damaged.

Cut Out Stencil Design *(Step 3)*

CUT OUT STENCILED SHAPES WITH A CRAFT KNIFE.

Transferring Stencil Design to Fabric

Supplies

Stencil

Cotton-jersey T-shirt or cotton-jersey fabric

Spray adhesive

Tools for your choice of stencil-transfer method *(see page 28)*

1. Prepare Work Surface

Cover your work surface with a sheet or towel to protect it and to keep your fabric stable when transferring your stencil. (At Alabama Chanin, we use old top sheets for this purpose. Over the years, they've been sprayed with so many different patterns and colors that they've become beautiful textiles in their own right; see right). Lay your fabric or T-shirt, right side up, on top of the protective material.

2. Protect T-Shirt

If you're working on a T-shirt, slip a piece of butcher paper or a scrap of fabric in between the front and the back of the shirt to prevent any marker or paint from seeping onto the back layer and ruining it before you even get started.

3. Prepare Stencil

Apply a light coating of spray adhesive on the back of your stencil to keep it from slipping during the transfer process.

4. Transfer Stencil Design on Fabric

Using your choice of stencil-transfer method, trace or fill in all the shapes cut out of your stencil.

Creating Large Allover Stencils

Sometimes you'll want to cover a fabric area larger than the actual size of your stencil. In this case, you'll need to use your stencil as a repeat to create a new, bigger allover stencil. We usually make our allover stencils 18" x 24", which is large enough to cover the body of most T-shirts.

Supplies

Stencil

18" x 24" tracing paper

Pen or pencil

18" x 24" poster board

Spray adhesive

Craft knife with sharp blade

1. Transfer One Repeat of Stencil Design on Tracing Paper

Lay the stencil in the center of the tracing paper. Trace around or fill in all the shapes of your design with a pen or pencil (see below).

2. Transfer Additional Repeats of Stencil Design on Tracing Paper

Move your stencil on the paper next to the design you just created, and trace or fill in the stencil design in its new position. Continue moving the stencil and retracing or filling it in until you've completely covered the paper, turning the design in different directions as you work to add interest (see below).

3. Cut Out Stencil Design

Once your page is covered with the stencil pattern, adhere the paper to poster board or felt with spray adhesive, and cut out each of the shapes of the extra-large stencil with a craft knife.

Creating Large Allover Stencils with Repeats *(Steps 1 and 2)*

Using Small Stencil to Make Larger Repeats

While a large stencil comes in handy for completely covering large areas, a small stencil can be manipulated to create interesting designs too. Follow the general directions on page 59 and the two steps here to create the repeat.

Supplies

Stencil

Cotton-jersey T-shirt or cotton-jersey fabric

Tools for transfer method of your choice *(see page 28)*

1. Place Stencil on Fabric and Trace First Repeat

Place your stencil on your fabric where you want your design to begin. (We usually work from the right shoulder seam down, following either the neckline or the armhole.) Transfer the stencil onto the fabric using your choice of transfer method.

2. Move Stencil and Trace Again to Create Larger Pattern

Pick up the stencil and place it near the first stenciled image, so elements of the new stenciled image look as if they're an extension of the first stenciled design (see below). Transfer the stencil again and again, as you like. Work in this way, "branching off" of the first stencil until you've covered the desired area. If using paint to transfer stencil, let the paint dry on both your shirt and the stencil before moving from one area to the next.

Using Small Stencil to Make Larger Repeats *(Step 1 and 2)*

Appliqué

Appliqué is a simple way of adding a decorative layer of fabric on top of a base fabric. Some textile historians believe that this technique may have originated in Egypt around 980 BC. Without a doubt it was long practiced in Europe; and the American artisans who brought it to the New World gave it their own voice and infused it with their own unique story. Appliqué enabled women to stitch memories into a quilt by adding a piece of fabric cut from a favorite piece of clothing and to document particular interests by appliquéing fabric cut into thematic shapes, such as flowers and plants.

Women in my community have been adorning their quilts with appliqué for generations; and, at Alabama Chanin, this is how we add different textures, colors, fabrics, and stories to our work. Appliqués can be stitched to the base fabric with invisible stitches or—as we like—with visible, decorative stitches.

Generally, a stencil is used to transfer a design for appliqué, but you don't have to use a stencil. Instead, you can draw or paint freehand and cut any shape from fabric to appliqué (or, for that matter, bypass drawing or painting and just freehand-cut shapes to appliqué).

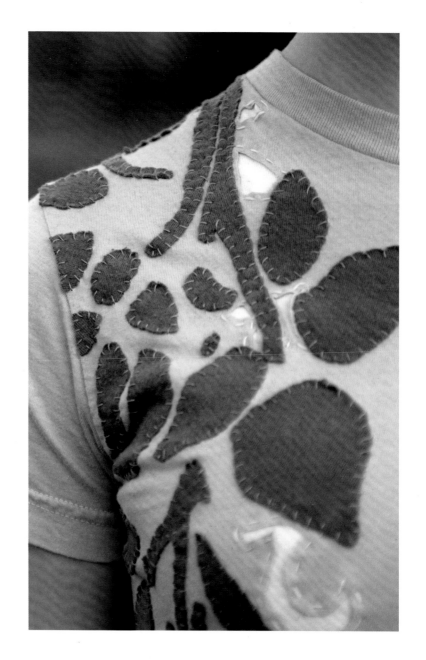

Directions for Appliqué

Supplies

Stencil

Base fabric for project

Fabric for appliqué pieces

Sharpie marker or textile spray paint

Pins

Needle

Buttonhole, craft, and carpet thread

Embroidery scissors

1. Stencil Pattern on Base Fabric

Stencil a pattern on the right side of your base fabric where you want to stitch your appliqué pieces (see page 59).

2. Cut Out Appliqué Pieces

To make your appliqué pieces, flip over the stencil you used in Step 1, and transfer the stencil pattern to the wrong side (back) of the appliqué fabric. When you cut out each shape of the stenciled pattern and flip it over right side up, it will fit exactly on the pattern that you stenciled on the base fabric.

3. Stitch Appliqué Pieces to Project

After cutting out each appliqué shape, place the cut piece on top of the corresponding shape in the pattern stenciled on your base fabric. Align the edges of the appliqué and stenciled shape, pin the appliqué securely in place, and attach the appliqué's raw cut edges using the stitch of your choice (see Chapter 3). The straight stitch is the easiest to use. The parallel whipstitch, which we used in the illustration below, is the most common and secures the fabric extremely well. Cross-stitch is a good decorative stitch for appliqué.

Stitch Appliqué to Project *(Step 3)*

APPLIQUÉS ATTACHED HERE WITH PARALLEL WHIPSTITCHES

Reverse Appliqué

When people think of reverse appliqué they often think of textiles called *molas* made by Kuna women on the coast of Panama. These colorful, intricate garments are made by sewing together layers of fabric (usually cotton) and then cutting through the various layers in patterns to reveal the variety of color below. The Hmong people of Vietnam are also known for similarly elaborate tone-on-tone designs. The quilt collection at the National Museum of American History includes a quilt embellished with reverse appliqué dated 1795, and some Baltimore album quilts from the mid-19th century feature spectacular reverse-appliqué borders.

When I first started experimenting with this technique, I must have had images of richly textured *molas* somewhere in the back of my mind. I began by reverse-appliquéing letters onto T-shirts and gradually expanded into more elaborate patterns. Today reverse-appliqué is Alabama Chanin's signature technique. We use it—usually in combination with stencils—to add depth and texture to a wide assortment of designs, ranging from book covers to evening gowns.

Our version of reverse appliqué begins with two layers of fabric. The top layer is stenciled and then stitched to the bottom layer by following the outline of the stenciled shapes. After stitching, we cut away the interior fabric within each shape to reveal the bottom fabric.

Directions for Reverse Appliqué

Supplies

Stencil

Fabric for top layer of project

Backing fabric in color different from top fabric and at least 1" larger than entire stenciled design

Sharpie marker or textile spray paint

Pins

Needle

Buttonhole, craft, and carpet thread

Embroidery scissors

1. Transfer Design to Top Fabric
Using a Sharpie marker or textile spray paint, transfer your stencil design on the right side of your cut top layer for your project.

2. Attach Backing Fabric to Top Fabric
Place the backing fabric, right side up, behind the area of the top layer of fabric to be appliquéd, making sure that the grain lines on both fabrics run in the same direction (see page 48). Pin the two fabrics together securely.

3. Stitch Around Stencil Shapes
Thread your needle with a double strand of thread, "love" your thread (see page 21), and knot off (see page 40). Choose one of the shapes in your stenciled design as a starting point, and

insert your needle according to the project directions, from either the right side of the top layer (in which case, your knot will show on the project's right side) or from the wrong side of the backing layer (in which case, the knot will be hidden inside the project), pulling the thread through the other layer. Then stitch around the shape using a straight stitch (see page 36) until you arrive back at your starting point, and knot off your thread using a double knot (see page 40) on the same side of the fabric as your starting knot. Move to a neighboring shape, and stitch around it, as before, tying off your thread with a double knot. Continue to move from one shape to the next, stitching around each one and tying off with a double knot. Always starting off with a fresh knot may seem like a lot of work, but it ensures that your garment will retain its stretch once it's complete.

4. Cut Away Top Layer Inside Stitched Shapes

Insert the tip of your embroidery scissors in the center of one of your stitched shapes, being careful to puncture *only* the top layer of fabric. Then carefully trim away the inside of the shape, leaving behind only $1/8$" of fabric alongside your stitched outline. The remaining $1/8$" is wide enough to prevent the fabric from unraveling and yet narrow enough to display the reverse appliqué pattern nicely (and a sliver of the original stenciled image's paint color). Make sure not to trim any closer than $1/8$" from your seam, which would cause the fabric to eventually tear away from the stitching.

Once you've trimmed the top layer of fabric on every shape, there are two options for finishing the backing fabric: either leave the fabric as is, or turn the project over or inside out and trim the backing to leave a narrow border around the entire piece. The directions in each project using reverse appliqué will tell you how to finish the backing layer.

Creating Reverse Appliqué *(Steps 1-4)*

1-2. STENCIL DESIGN ON TOP LAYER, AND PLACE BACKING LAYER UNDERNEATH.

3. STITCH AROUND EACH STENCILED SHAPE.

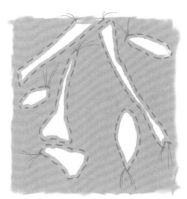

4. TRIM INTERIOR OF EACH SHAPE, STOPPING $1/8$" FROM STITCHES, TO REVEAL BACKING FABRIC.

3-D Appliqué

Three-dimensional, or 3-D appliqué, simply combines standard appliqué and reverse appliqué to create a 3-D effect. The key thing to remember when stenciling designs for the appliqué part of 3-D is that you need to flip the stencil over to its wrong side to transfer the stencil design onto the appliqué fabric. This produces a mirror-image of the regular stencil design that will fit correctly, once turned right side up, over the stencil design already transferred to the base fabric. After you position the 3-D appliqué right side up over the base fabric's design, you're ready to attach the appliqué with whipstitches or any other stitch you like (see page 36).

3-D Appliqué

REVERSE APPLIQUÉ   APPLIQUÉ

Tips for Appliqué and Reverse Appliqué

• When working with reverse appliqué on a T-shirt, it can be difficult to get the backing fabric pinned flat inside the T-shirt. To make it easier, turn the T-shirt inside out, pin the backing fabric in place, then turn the T-shirt right side out for stitching.

• Stitcher Diane Hall has a good suggestion for beginning sewers who are afraid of puncturing both layers of fabric when trimming the top-layer fabric from the shapes in their stenciled design: After transferring the stencil design but before applying the backing fabric and stitching around the individual stencil shapes, make a small cut in the center of each stenciled shape. This will give you a place to start when you're ready to trim away the fabric from each shape. Just make sure that your initial cut does not go beyond the $\frac{1}{8}$" boundary at the edge of your stenciled shape.

• For very small ($\frac{1}{4}$" or smaller) stencil shapes, don't clip away the fabric. Just leave the stitched shape as is, so it becomes yet another decorative texture.

Beading

People have adorned clothing with beads and other embellishments since ancient times. In America, the Colonists found an indigenous culture that decorated clothing with handmade shell, bone, and semiprecious-stone beads. Only after trade opened up with Europe did the Colonists have access to glass beads.

The beaded garments in the Alabama Chanin collections are among our clients' favorites. Some T-shirts may have as few as three or four beads, or a skirt that's heavily embellished may hold up to ten thousand beads.

Adding beads to a project gives it texture and shine. Beading can also accentuate or outline a design element like an appliqué rose. A simple way to use beads is "seam-beading" (as you straight-stitch your seams, add a bead to each stitch). On page 31, you'll find a lot of other strategies for beading.

You can bead either a single layer of fabric or multiple layers. Regardless of whether the added layer (or layers) is appliquéd on top of the base fabric or positioned behind it (as for reverse appliqué), the multiple layers are treated as a unit, that is, as a single layer. Hence, the beading process for both single- and multi-layer fabrics is the same and is described below.

Adding Beads to a Project

Supplies
Glass bugle beads or seed beads
Buttonhole, carpet, and craft thread
Millinery needle with large eye

1. Preparing to Bead
Thread the beading needle, love your thread (see page 21), and knot off (see page 40).

2. Beading Your Work
Insert the needle into either the fabric's right or wrong side, depending on whether or not you want the knot to show on the project's right side. Take one stitch, bringing your needle up to the right side; insert your needle through a bead; and take another stitch, again bringing your needle up on the right side. Continue inserting your needle through a bead (or two or three, depending on how many will fit on the size of your stitch), stitching, and pulling your thread through to right side of the fabric.

The project directions in this book provide specific instructions for beading, but the number of beads you use is solely up to you. You can place one or more beads on every stitch, every other stitch, every fifth (for example) stitch; or you can place beads randomly throughout your project. The decisions and creativity belong to you.

Beading Tips

The key to beading is to get a good rhythm going. Here are some strategies:

• Stitcher Shelby Wade puts her beads in a plastic tray and dips her needle right into the tray to nab a bead. "It's kind of like fishing," she says.

• Another method is to put double-sided tape around the top of your index finger on your free hand—or even on your pants leg—and put a pile of beads on the sticky surface. Then you simply pick up the beads with the needle as you need them, and continue on your stitching way.

• A beading glove is a great device to aid in beading. See page 99 for instructions on making stitcher Wanita Lawler's ingenious glove.

CHAPTER 5 | Projects

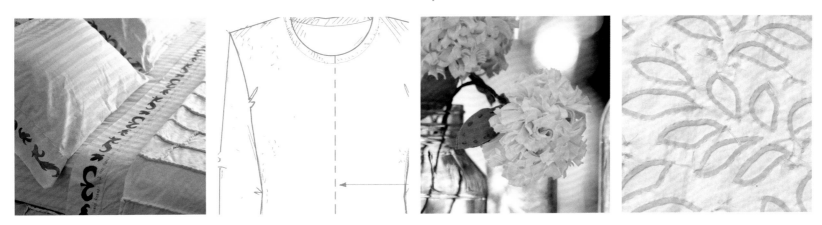

Now that you know the techniques used in this book, you're ready to begin stitching. The projects presented here are modern interpretations of classic designs. They are at once beautiful, functional, and durable. As you use your own hands and vision to make them, you will be creating a unique, personal story. You'll soon discover that a handmade item stitched by someone who loves what they do has an unmistakably soulful quality. You'll also have the satisfaction of knowing that you are creating something for the next generation. And the next. And the next.

Bloomers Shirt

A pair of scissors, needle, and thread can transform any garment into a custom piece that fits your unique body type and says something about your individual sense of style. In 2000, when I began my work with recycled clothing, I made my first cut into a T-shirt and stitched it back together. Since then, the more I stitch, the more I realize that design is not lofty and untouchable. It belongs to all of us.

But making the first cut is difficult. Taking that first step to do anything new, like starting a business or taking up stitching, can be filled with doubt and fear. If I've learned anything from building the business of Alabama Chanin, it's that the reality of our fears is rarely as bad as we envision and that fear only serves to get in the way of the important things that we need to do.

My Design Choice | T-shirt - Faded pink

Supplies

Long-sleeved cotton-jersey T-shirt

Bloomers stencil *(see pullout after page 144)*

Garment scissors

Tailor's chalk or disappearing-ink fabric pen

Spray adhesive

Sharpie marker

Favorite decorative pin or safety pin

Cut Open Center Front of T-Shirt *(Step 1)*

CUTTING LINE

1. Cut Open Center Front of T-Shirt

Determine the center front of your T-shirt by folding the garment in half, with the sleeves positioned at the sides, and carefully measuring in from the sides. Using the garment scissors, cut through the top layer only of the T-shirt from the bottom edge up through the neckline (see left).

2. Stencil Design on T-Shirt

Note: You may want to practice this step on a piece of scrap cotton jersey before you work on your T-shirt. Open up your cut T-shirt, and lay out the front right panel, with the right side facing up, on a clean work surface. (Laying your T-shirt on an old sheet, a flat piece of fabric, or a small towel will help hold the T-shirt in place as you stencil the design on it and will also protect your work surface.) Spray a light coating of spray adhesive on the back of your Bloomers stencil to keep it firmly in place, and position it carefully over the the area of the T-shirt that you want to decorate. Using the Sharpie marker, carefully trace around each individual cut-out shape in the stencil on the front of the T-shirt (see photos on page 72). Repeat this process on the back shoulder or wherever else you want.

3. Add Message

Decide what words or poetry you want to write on your T-shirt. You may want to first figure out the spacing of the words using a disappearing-ink pen or tailor's chalk (always test in an inconspicuous place on your fabric, like the inside back hem, beforehand to make sure the marks will actually disappear). The goal is for the words to begin and end at the T-shirt's center-front bottom edge, crossing both side seams and filling the entire bottom edge all around. If you think you may need to practice spacing your words more than once, make a paper test strip or two by measuring the full length of your bottom edge and the height you plan to make your words and then cutting the test strips to these dimensions.

After figuring out the word spacing, using the Sharpie marker and beginning at the right front panel, write your message freehand across the bottom of the shirt.

4. Close T-Shirt with a Favorite Pin

Put on the stenciled T-shirt, and pin the front closed with a favorite pin or simply a safety pin.

Sequin Appliqués

Sequin appliqués are a good way to add detail to the Bloomers Shirt or other garments. However, because these appliqués are usually attached simply to a thin piece of starched gauze, they tend to break apart after the first washing if you don't stitch them down strategically. At Alabama Chanin, we stitch every third outside sequin as well as every third sequin in the middle of the appliqué, as shown below in red.

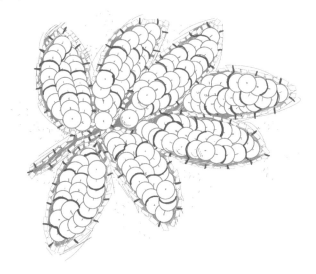

Stenciled Sheets

When one of my good friends moved into her new house, I wanted to find something personal for her housewarming gift. After thinking about what makes a house a home, I remembered how my great grandmother used to tat lace for our pillowcases and bedding. It was her way of making simple, ordinary textiles special for her family. She also tatted her beautiful lace as housewarming presents for friends and neighbors.

Those memories inspired me to buy some crisp cotton sheets and decorate them for my friend. At the time, I had not yet learned to tat my own lace, so I decided to use one of our lace-inspired stencils. I have used this technique many times since then to make sheets for myself, other friends, and family. I like to customize these presents by hand-writing stories on each set. The stories can be a simple children's nursery rhyme or a dream that's vividly remembered. It is said that we spend a quarter of our life in bed, so why not make that time extraordinary?

My Design Choices

Sheet — Butter
Paint — Dark red
Drawing tool — Extra-fine black Sharpie marker

Supplies

One set of 100-percent cotton sheets
(or recycle a set from your linen closet)

Lace Stripe stencil *(see below)*

Poster board or felt *(see page 28)*, 4" larger all around
than finished Lace Stripe

Spray adhesive

Craft knife with sharp blade

Spray adhesive

Textile paint for transferring stencil *(see page 28)*

Sharpie marker

1. Prepare and Cut Stencil

Photocopy the Lace Stripe stencil below, increasing or
decreasing its size to suit the sheets you're working with. For
the sheets shown here, the stencil graphic was enlarged by
300 percent. Following the instructions for making a stencil
on page 58, prepare your Lace Stripe stencil.

2. Customize Sheets by Stenciling Design

Open your top sheet and lay it flat on a clean working surface,
right side up (laying the sheet you're going to stencil on top of
an old sheet or a flat piece of fabric and/or weighting the ends
of the sheet will help keep it in place as you start to draw and
will also protect your work surface). Spray a light coating of
spray adhesive on the back of the Lace Stripe stencil to keep it
firmly in place, and position the stencil carefully on the left edge
of the sheet's top border. Using textile paint, carefully transfer the
stencil on to the sheet's border, making sure to cover each
individual shape in the stencil design. When you've finished
painting the entire stencil, let the transferred image and stencil
dry. Then remove the stencil and reposition it adjacent to the
first stenciled motif, and transfer the design again. Repeat
this process until you've completely stenciled the entire border.
If you want to stencil the fitted sheet or the borders of the
pillowcases, repeat the process on each item.

3. Trace Stenciled Design

Using a Sharpie marker, trace around the outside edge of each
shape in your stenciled design. Then add a message or a poem
below it using the Sharpie marker.

Lace Stripe Stencil *(Step 1)*

Note: For projects in this book, the Lace Stripe Stencil was enlarged by 300 percent.

That I lived in the *north* *...*

Getting a Grip

I think nonstick, gripping shelf liner, which is sold in rolls in most grocery stores, makes a great work surface. Because of its nonslip properties, it keeps pens, tools, and spools of thread from rolling away; and you can even stick your extra pins and needles into its soft surface, so they don't fall on the floor or in your lap as you work. It also buffers the sound of your scissors hitting the hard table surface as you put them down and pick them up while stitching.

When I grew up, biscuits were always part of any good country breakfast, and there was never a morning without them. I learned to make them from my mother and grandmothers, who baked them every day as a side dish to eggs, bacon, country-fried steak, and grits. These days, I often make biscuits the breakfast centerpiece, cutting them with shaped cookie cutters into little stars, and serving them with freshly cooked fruits and whipped cream or butter and honey. Here's my son Zach's favorite recipe:

Biscuits

1 stick (8 tablespoons) cold salted butter, plus extra for serving

2 cups self-rising flour

Approximately ¾ cup cold whole milk

Cookie cutters in various shapes

1. Preheat the oven to 425°F.
2. Cut the butter into the flour using a pastry cutter (cold ingredients help make biscuits fluffy).
3. Add milk while stirring, until the mixture sticks together but is moist. Turn the dough onto a floured surface.
4. Knead the dough lightly until it holds together.
5. Flatten and roll the dough lightly with a rolling pin to 1" in height.
6. Fold the rolled dough in half, and roll it out lightly again. Repeat this six to eight times.
7. Use cookie cutters to cut a variety of shaped biscuits.
8. Shape the last remaining dough (which won't be enough to use with a cutter) by hand—these are what we call "cat head" biscuits in my family, and they're always everyone's favorites.
9. Place biscuits on a baking sheet and bake for approximately 10 minutes or until golden brown.
10. Serve with butter.

Reverse-Appliqué Bandana

This bandana is the first project our stitchers make. It's their "audition" piece, and it allows them to practice or show off their stitching expertise. But this is an easy project that anyone, at any skill level, can make, wear, and enjoy. We created the bandana's decorative pattern using reverse appliqué, which is one of our signature techniques.

When I first came back to Alabama and put out the call for experienced stitchers, the response was overwhelming. As a result, we found ourselves with hundreds of bandanas, and we didn't know what to do with them. Then it occurred to us to donate them to cancer patients in our area. This is now a tradition.

We're always touched to receive notes from bandana recipients, who are grateful that someone wanted to take time to create a handmade, one-of-a-kind gift. I hope you will invite friends to join you in stitching bandanas for the charity of your choice. In the vein of old-style quilting circles, community-minded work simply makes the process more enriching.

My Design Choices		Version 1	Version 2
	Top fabric	– Pink	Cream
	Backing fabric	– Cream	Blue
	Paint	– Gold	Tan
	Thread	– Cream	Brown
	Knots	– Positioned on right side for Version 1, on wrong side for Version 2	

Supplies

Two cotton-jersey T-shirts, in different colors

One 20" square and one 16" square of pattern paper *(for paper options, see page 23)*

Bloomers stencil *(see pullout after page 144)*

Garment scissors

Embroidery scissors

Transparent plastic ruler

Tailor's chalk or disappearing-ink fabric pen

Tools for your choice of stencil-transfer method *(see page 28)*

Pins

Needle

Buttonhole, carpet, and craft thread

Make Pattern *(Step 1)*

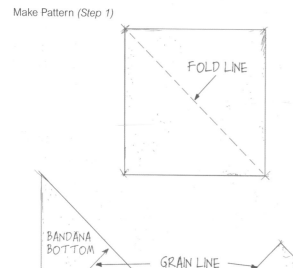

1. Make Pattern

Fold your 20" square of pattern paper in half, aligning the two opposite corners to create a large triangle measuring 20" x 20" x 28½". Fold this pattern piece in half again to establish your grain line, and label the fold line "Grain Line" and the entire triangle "Bandana Bottom."

Repeat this process with your 16" square pattern to create a triangle measuring 16" x 16" x 23". Fold this piece in half again to establish your grain line, and label that fold line "Grain Line" and this triangle "Bandana Top."

2. Prepare for Cutting

Deconstruct your two T-shirts (see page 48), so you have a sleeveless tube of fabric separated at the shoulder seams. Cut each tube from the bottom edge below the center of one armhole straight up to the armhole, so the tube can lie flat as a single layer.

3. Cut Out Two Bandana Pieces

Decide which deconstructed T-shirt to use for the Bandana Bottom, and lay your Bandana Bottom pattern on that T-shirt, making sure the marked grain line runs in the same direction as the T-shirt's grain line (see page 48). Using tailor's chalk, trace around your pattern's edges, and remove the pattern. Cut out your Bandana Bottom just inside the chalked line to remove all the chalk.

Lay your Bandana Top pattern on your second deconstructed T-shirt, and repeat the process to cut out the piece.

4. Stencil Design on Bandana Top

Lay your Bandana Top, right side up (see page 48), and place your Bloomers stencil on top of it. Using your choice of stencil-transfer method, transfer the stencil design on the Bandana Top, then move it to an adjacent spot and again transfer the design (if you're transferring the stencil with paint, let the paint on the fabric and stencil dry before transferring the design again). Continue moving and tracing the stencil until the design covers the entire Bandana Top.

5. Pin Bandana Top and Bottom Together

Center and pin the Bandana Top on the Bandana Bottom, with the right side of each fabric facing up. Make sure the top's edges are equidistant from the edges of the bottom.

Prepare for Stitching *(Step 5)*

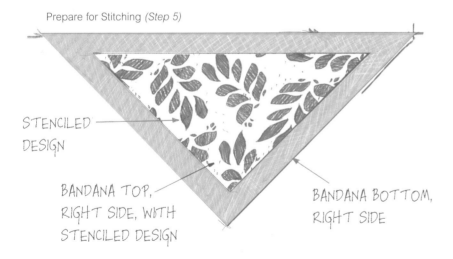

STENCILED DESIGN

BANDANA TOP, RIGHT SIDE, WITH STENCILED DESIGN

BANDANA BOTTOM, RIGHT SIDE

6. Stitch Stenciled Shapes

Thread your needle, "love" your thread (see page 21), and knot off (see page 40). Begin stitching on the edge of any stenciled shape on the Bandana Top, inserting your needle either down or up through both layers. Bring your needle back up or down to the top or bottom and, using a straight stitch (see page 36), work around the shape's edge. Knot off on the top, move on to a neighboring shape, and repeat the process, keeping all of the knots on either the top or bottom. Stitch around all the stenciled shapes this way. When stitching the stenciled shapes at the edge of your Bandana Top, leave the actual edge of the top unstitched because you'll trim this fabric away. Stitch only on top of transferred lines, tying a knot at the end of each shape.

7. Cut Reverse Appliqué

Following the reverse-appliqué instructions on page 64, separate the two layers and use embroidery scissors to clip through the top layer only inside one stitched shape. Trim the top fabric from the shape's interior, stopping $1/8"$ away from your stitching line. Continue to trim away the top fabric from all the inner areas of each stitched shape until you've trimmed all the shapes.

Cutting the Reverse Appliqué *(Step 7)*

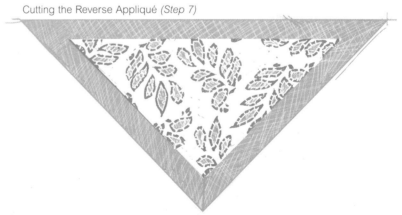

Rooter Shirt

When I first came back to Alabama, I started making shirts using rooster stencils. This farm animal seemed to speak to the lifestyle this rural environment inspired—reconnecting with the land, fresh air, clean fun, good food, and rising early to begin the day.

The Rooster stencil used here was created for a series of T-shirt designs that we laughingly call "farm animals and wildlife." We've used stencils of pigs, eagles, flies, bees, and beetles; and all of them have become part of our larger stencil library. We revisit these images from time to time, and consequently they've become classics for us.

For this project, you can use the basic reverse-appliqué technique called for in the directions; but as your skill set grows, you may want to add other embroidery or appliqué techniques as embellishment.

My Design Choices

T-shirt	– Blue
Backing fabric	– Red
Paint	– Red
Thread	– Red

Supplies

Cotton-jersey T-shirt in any color

12" square of scrap jersey for backing fabric
(or as large as you want your rooster to be)

Rooster stencil *(see below)*

Poster board or felt *(see page 28)*, 4" larger all around than finished rooster's size

Spray adhesive

Craft knife with sharp blade

Tools for your choice of stencil-transfer method *(see page 28)*

Butcher paper, pattern paper, or newspaper *(see page 23)*

Cutting mat

Garment scissors

Embroidery scissors

Pins

Needle

Buttonhole, carpet, and craft thread

Rooster Stencil *(Step 1)*

Note: For projects in this book, the Rooster stencil was enlarged by 455 percent.

1. Prepare and Cut Stencil

Make a photocopy or scan and print out the Rooster stencil below, adjusting its size to suit your T-shirt. For the T-shirt shown here, we enlarged the stencil by 455 percent. Following instructions on page 58, prepare your Rooster stencil.

2. Transfer Stencil to T-Shirt

Following the stencil-transfer instructions on page 58, place your prepared Rooster stencil on the T-shirt, and transfer the graphic to your T-shirt.

3. Add Reverse-Appliqué Fabric

Carefully pin your scrap-jersey backing fabric on the inside of your T-shirt behind the stenciled rooster, making sure the grain lines on the scrap fabric and the T-shirt run in the same direction (see page 48) and that the right side of the backing fabric faces the wrong side of the T-shirt.

4. Stitch Around Stenciled Shapes

Thread your needle, "love" your thread (see page 21), and knot off (see page 40). Begin stitching one of the stenciled shapes from your Rooster stencil by inserting your needle down through the right side of your T-shirt and through the backing fabric, leaving the knot visible on the right side of your T-shirt. Bring your needle back up to the right side of the T-shirt and, using a straight stitch (see page 36), sew around the outer edge of the shape. When you've stitched around the entire shape, knot off your thread on the right side, then stitch around the next shape in the same way. Continue stitching all the elements in the Rooster design, following guidelines for reverse appliqué on page 64.

5. Cut the Reverse Appliqué

Following the instructions for reverse appliqué, carefully separate the two layers of one reverse-appliquéd shape, and use your embroidery scissors to clip through the top layer only. Insert your scissors into this clipped slit, and trim away the entire inside of the shape, stopping $\frac{1}{8}$" from your stitching line. Repeat the process to trim the other reverse-appliquéd shapes. Turn the shirt inside out, and trim away the extra backing fabric around the entire stenciled design, trimming to about $\frac{1}{4}$" from the stitches on the design's outer perimeter.

Bleaching

Sometimes I use bleach (sparingly) to change the colors of recycled shirts and to create patterns in the fabric. The process below is easy—and most of us have done it at least one time by accident(!). In the photo at left and on page 86, you can clearly see the pattern made by bleaching.

1. Fill your washing machine with hot water.

2. Add T-shirts along with the desired amount of laundry detergent.

3. Agitate the wash for 2 minutes.

4. Open the washing machine's lid, and let the T-shirts soak for 20 minutes.

5. Pour in 1 cup bleach, and let the garments soak for another 20 minutes.

6. Wash as normal.

Note: It's very important to use this technique with caution because bleach can burn a hole in fabric and permanently damage the fibers. Also remember that bleach is caustic to both the skin and the environment. Always use it sparingly, cautiously, and with Mother Nature in mind.

Tea Towels

Tea towels were originally handmade linen cloths specifically designed for English ladies to use to dry their teapots and cups after washing them. With the advent of the Industrial Revolution and textile manufacturing, machine-made versions of these towels became readily available, and consequently they became a more "disposable" item. However, women like my grandmothers still chose to make their own. I have inherited some of their tea towels, which they made from flour sacks they cut into rectangles, embroidered, and beautifully finished on the edges. My grandmothers used these towels in bread baskets, as tray liners, and as little gifts for friends and neighbors. One of my grandfathers used one of these towels as his napkin at just about every meal of his married life.

After years of working with cotton jersey, we've learned that it is a great material for everything from garments to cleaning rags. I don't use these handmade tea towels as cleaning rags, but they're wonderful to use in the kitchen, both for drying dishes and as oversized napkins.

		Version 1	Version 2
My Design Choices	Top fabric	– White	Burnt Orange
	Backing fabric	– Cream	Red
	Paint	– Beige	Dark Red
	Thread	– Cream	Red
	Knots	– Positioned on back of towel	

Supplies

Two cotton-jersey T-shirts or cotton-jersey scraps in two different colors

One 19" x 26" piece and one 4" x 19" piece of pattern paper *(for paper options, see page 23)*

Lace Stripe stencil *(see page 78)*

Garment scissors

Embroidery scissors

Transparent plastic ruler

Tailor's chalk or disappearing-ink fabric pen

Tools needed for your choice of stencil-transfer method *(see page 28)*

Seam ripper

Pins

Needle

Buttonhole, carpet, and craft thread

Create Patterns *(Step 1)*

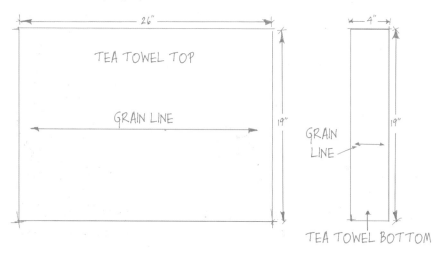

1. Create Patterns and Stencil

On your 19" x 26" piece of pattern paper, draw a straight line parallel to the paper's long side, and label this line "Grain Line" and the entire pattern piece "Tea Towel Top."

On your 4" x 19" piece of pattern paper, draw a straight line parallel to the paper's short side, and label this line "Grain Line" and the entire pattern piece "Tea Towel Bottom."

Photocopy the Lace Stripe stencil, enlarging it by 300 percent. Prepare and cut the stencil according to the instructions on page 58.

2. Prepare Cotton-Jersey for Cutting

Deconstruct the two T-shirts, as explained on page 48 so that you have a sleeveless tube of fabric separated at the shoulder seams. Cut from the bottom left side of each tube straight up to the center of the left armhole so that the tube opens out completely to lie flat as a single layer.

3. Cut Out Tea-Towel Pieces

Decide which T-shirt fabric you want to use for the Tea Towel Top, and lay your Tea Towel Top pattern on top of that fabric, making sure the pattern's marked grain line runs in the same direction as the T-shirt's grain line (see page 48). Using tailor's chalk, trace around the pattern's edges, then remove the pattern. Cut out your Tea Towel Top, cutting just inside the chalked line to remove all the chalk. Lay your Tea Towel Bottom pattern on the second deconstructed T-shirt, and cut as above. Repeat the process, so you have two Tea Towel Bottom pieces. Set aside T-shirt scraps for a future project.

4. Stencil Design on Tea-Towel Top

Lay your Tea Towel Top with the right side of the fabric (see page 48) facing up. Place your Lace Stripe stencil on your Tea Towel Top ½" from the top short edge. Using your choice of stencil-transfer method, carefully transfer the stencil design on to the Tea Towel Top, stenciling all the way from one side edge of the fabric to the other. Reposition the stencil 2" from the top edge, and repeat the stenciling process for the second stripe.

Repeat the stenciling process at other end of the tea towel if you want.

Stencil Design *(Step 4)*

5. Add Reverse-Appliqué Fabric

Carefully pin your Tea Towel Bottom, with the right side facing up, on the wrong side of your Tea Towel Top behind the stenciled Lace Stripe. Make sure that the grain lines on the top and bottom of the tea towel run in the same direction.

6. Stitch Around Stenciled Shapes

Thread your needle, "love" your thread (see page 21), and knot off (see page 40). Begin stitching right on the edge of one of the stenciled shapes by inserting your needle from the wrong side of the Tea Towel Bottom up through the Tea Towel Top (your knot will show on the wrong side of the Tea Towel Bottom). Using a straight stitch (see page 36), sew around the edge of the stenciled shape. When you arrive back where you started stitching, knot off and cut the thread on the wrong side of the Tea Towel Bottom. Then knot your thread again, and start stitching around the next shape, as you did with the first one. Continue stitching around each remaining stenciled shape, following the directions and tips for reverse appliqué on page 64.

7. Cut Reverse Appliqué

Following the instructions for reverse appliqué, carefully separate the two layers of one of the reverse-appliquéd shapes, and use your embroidery scissors to clip into the top layer only. Insert your scissors into this clipped slit, and trim away the entire inside of the shape, stopping ⅛" from the stitching line. Continue trimming the interior of all the shapes in your stencil design.

One day when I was feeling a bit down, my friend Jen Rausch called. She told me I was allowed 20 minutes of self-pity, but then I was to get up and get on with my work. A few hours later, Jen arrived at the office with a tray lined with a beautiful tea towel, which held a china bowl, a jar of warm soup, and some homemade whole-wheat crackers. I will always be grateful to Jen for that sweet gesture.

The tea towels on page 91 are perfect for such a moment. You can include Jen's crackers and a jar of my friend Ms. Jessie's vegetable soup. Ms. Jessie got the recipe from a Depression-era government pamphlet, and she makes about 20 jars a year, most of which she gives away. Ms. Jessie once told me, "Peoples is going in different directions now. They don't even get together to eat a meal." Take the opportunity to share that pleasure.

Jen's Whole-Wheat Crackers

3/4 cup vegetable oil

1 cup water

3 cups quick oats

2 cups whole-wheat flour

1 cup wheat germ

2 tablespoons sugar

1/2 teaspoon salt

Preheat the oven to about 300° to 325°F. Blend or beat the liquid ingredients, and pour them over the dry ingredients in a bowl. Mix, then roll out the dough on the bottom of two large baking sheets to the edges. Sprinkle with salt, and cut into 2" squares. Bake for about 30-40 minutes or until crisp and golden brown.

Yield: Makes about forty 2"-square crackers.

Ms. Jessie's Vegetable Soup

1 quart water

2 gallons ripe tomatoes, peeled and cut into quarters

16 ears corn, with kernels cut off

4 green bell peppers, chopped

4 medium onions, chopped

2 hot pepper pods, chopped

1 package carrots, diced

2 cans English peas

2 cans lima beans

1/2 cup vinegar

1 cup sugar

1/3 cup salt

Mix together all the vegetables with the quart of water in a large canner. Add the vinegar, sugar, and salt. Bring to a boil, and cook 45 minutes. Pour into clean jars, and seal the jars with Kerr or Ball lids and rings. Don't tighten the lids too much. Put the filled jars into an empty canner with a rack on bottom, then add enough hot water to cover the top of the hot jars completely. Bring to a hard boil, then cook at least 35-40 minutes. Remove the canner from the heat onto the top of the stove; let the jars sit in the canner 15-20 minutes until they can be removed from the hot water.

Alternatively, if you don't want to use a canner, cook the soup for 30 minutes; then cool and freeze.

Yield: Makes about 7 quarts (or halve the recipe to make enough for 6 people).

Beaded Postcard

I've collected postcards since I was a little girl. Whenever anyone goes on a trip, I ask them to send me a postcard; and, consequently, I now have about two thousand cards from all over the world. Postcards celebrate nostalgia, keep the past alive for us in the present, and provide a vicarious trip to a place we may one day want to visit.

In fact, I have a postcard table set up in my house, and I often cut up old images or pictures and embroider and bead them to make my own small collages. People have been customizing postcards since as early as 1906, when Eastman Kodak released a camera that took postcard-sized photographs that could be processed on postcard paper. Today, making your own one-of-a-kind postcards is a great way to reclaim and recycle any image or scrap of paper that you like.

I send beaded cards, like the one shown here, for special occasions or as thank-you's to all the people who have helped me along the way. I really like making cards because they inspire me to slow down and think about what I've enjoyed most about a dinner party, a gift, or just spending time with someone I care about.

My Design Choices

Paper — Brown kraft cardstock
Thread . — Tan
Bugle bead — Light pink

Supplies

Postcard (*see pullout after page 144*)

Beading needle, size #10

Buttonhole, carpet, and craft thread

Eighty #4 bugle beads

Start Beading *(Step 2)*

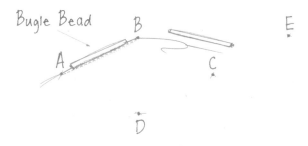

1. Down at A, up at B, insert bugle bead.
2. Down at A, up at B, insert bugle bead.
3. Down at C, up at D, insert bugle bead.
4. Down at A, up at D, insert bugle bead.
5. Down at C, up at E; repeat to create next diamond.

1. Choose Beads

Choose your beads and test the bead size with a threaded needle. Although some needles will pass through a given bead when unthreaded, the added dimension of the thread sometimes prevents the needle from fitting through the bead's hole, so it's useful to check before starting your project.

2. Start Beading

Remove the pullout postcard. Thread your needle, "love" your thread (see page 21), and knot it off (see page 40). Insert your threaded needle into the front top left corner of the card through the first hole labeled "A" (see the drawing at left), then pull the thread through to the back of the card. Insert your needle from the back, come up through B, and add a bugle bead. Next work Steps 2–5 noted below the drawing to complete the first diamond, adding a bead each time before inserting your needle from the front to the back of the card. Keep working this way until you've completed one edge of the card, and knot off your thread. Repeat the process for the three remaining edges.

Beading Glove

For a while some of our stitchers were using double-stick tape on their hands to keep their beads close to their fabric. But days of beading a project, constantly pulling the tape off and putting it back on again, left the skin on their hands raw. To fix the problem, stitcher Wanita Lawler came up with this ingenious beading glove.

1. Cut a 3" x 6" rectangle from ribbing fabric (cut off the wrist, neck, or bottom edge of deconstructed T-shirt; see page 48), making sure to cut the rectangle so that the fabric's grain line runs parallel to the 3" side.

2. Fold the ribbing in half with wrong sides together, so it now measures 3" square.

3. Stitch the raw edges opposite the fold together ¼" from the edge. Fold the seam allowances over to one side, and stitch them down with a felled seam (see page 44).

4. Lay the stitched tube flat, with the seam at one side. On the folded edge opposite the seam, measure 1" down from the top edge, and cut a ½"-wide slit towards the seam through both layers.

5. Put your hand in the glove and your thumb through the slit. Add double-sided tape to the top of the glove. Sprinkle beads on top of the tape, and stitch away.

MORE POSTCARD PATTERNS

Here are some additional postcard stitching patterns to choose from. Photocopy these pages, enlarging them 130 percent (in order to create a 5½" x 4¾" postcard, as shown); cut out the individual patterns, and paper-clip the pattern you want to use to the cardstock, making sure that the two layers are aligned. Using a straight pin or a safety pin, punch a hole through both layers at each black dot. If you want, place the aligned pattern and cardstock on top of a small piece of corrugated cardboard or foam core to avoid making holes in your work surface. Always double-check the alignment of your pattern before you start punching your holes.

- Seed Bead

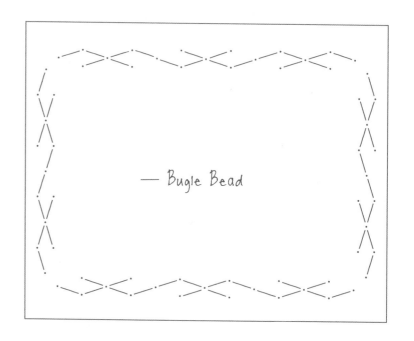

— Bugle Bead

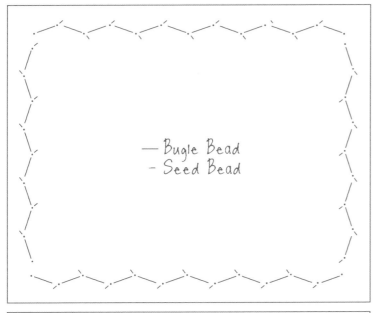

—Bugle Bead
- Seed Bead

—Bugle Bead
- Seed Bead

—Bugle Bead
- Seed Bead

- Seed Bead

Lace-Stripe Headband

Hair ornamentation has taken many forms throughout history—from the plumes and powders of Marie Antoinette to the beads and shells of African women. Hair comes and goes; gets cut, then grows back; is black (or brown or blond) and then one day grey like mine. It's an ever-changing cycle, but there's always a reason to adorn it, whether you're suffering from a bad hair day or you just want to accessorize. For my very first runway show, I made headbands like this one for the models to wear. It's an easy project to complete, and you'll see that it can be developed in many different ways.

My Design Choices

Top fabric	– White
Backing fabric	– White
Paint	– Grey
Thread	– Cream
Beads	– Rose seed beads

Supplies

One cotton-jersey T-shirt or cotton-jersey scraps

Two pieces of pattern paper, 2¾" x 16" and 2¾" x 12"
(for different paper options, see page 23)

Lace Stripe stencil *(see page 78)*

Garment scissors

Embroidery scissors

Transparent plastic ruler

Tailor's chalk or disappearing-ink fabric pen

Tools for your choice of stencil-transfer method *(see page 28)*

Ultra-fine-point Sharpie marker

Pins

Sewing needle

Millinery needle

Buttonhole, carpet, and craft thread

Approximately 500 seed beads

1. Create Pattern and Stencil

On your 2¾" x 16" pattern paper, draw a line parallel to the short 2¾" side, and label this line "Grain Line" and the pattern piece itself "Headband."

On your 2¾" x 12" pattern paper, draw a line parallel to the 2¾" side and label this line "Grain Line." On the opposite 2¾" end, measure in ¾" from the top and bottom of this end and connect these points with the top and bottom of the other 2¾" end, producing a tapered shape (officially called a trapezoid) that's 2¾" on one end and 1¼" on the other (see the illustration below). Label this pattern piece "Headband Tie."

Photocopy the Lace Stripe stencil, enlarging it by 300 percent. Prepare and cut the stencil according to the instructions on page 58.

2. Prepare Fabric

Deconstruct your T-shirt (see page 48), so you have a sleeveless tube of fabric that's separated at the shoulder seams. Then cut the tube from the bottom edge below the center of one armhole straight up to that center armhole, so the tube can open out and lie flat as a single layer.

Create Pattern Pieces for Headband and Ties *(Step 1)*

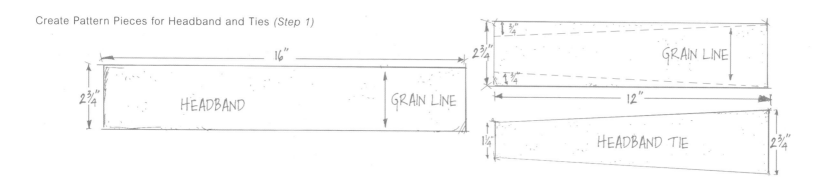

3. Cut Out Two Headband Pieces

Lay your Headband pattern on top of the T-shirt fabric laid flat as a single layer, making sure the pattern's marked grain line runs in the same direction as the fabric's grain line (see page 48). With tailor's chalk, trace around the pattern's edges, remove the pattern, and cut out the headband, making sure to cut in a smooth line just inside the chalked line to remove it entirely. Repeat this process, so you have two headband pieces, one for the top and one for the bottom.

Lay your Headband Tie pattern piece on the remaining T-shirt fabric, and repeat the process above to cut out two ties for your headband.

4. Stencil Design on Headband

Lay one headband piece, with the fabric's right side up (see page 48) on your work surface. Place the Lace Stripe stencil in the center of the headband. Using your choice of stencil-transfer method, carefully transfer the stencil onto the headband. Then lift the stencil and move it to transfer the image as needed to cover the entire headband. If you used paint to transfer the stencil, let the stenciled fabric and the stencil itself dry before moving the stencil to make additional stencil transfers.

5. Pin Headband Top and Bottom Together and Align Sides

Center the stenciled headband piece on the top of the second headband piece, with the right side of both fabrics facing up. Align the edges of both fabrics, and pin the two pieces together.

6. Stitch Inside Stenciled Shapes

Thread your needle, "love" your thread (see page 21), and knot off (see page 40). Begin stitching ⅛" in from the edge of one stenciled shape on the headband by inserting your needle

down through the two headband layers, so your knot shows on the top of the headband. Bring your needle back up to the top, and, using a beaded back stitch (see page 37), sew around the shape ⅛" from the edge of the stenciled shape, picking up one bead on each stitch. When you arrive back where you started stitching, knot off your thread on the top of the headband. Then move on to stitch around the next shape in the same way. Continue stitching until you've outlined all the shapes with stitches.

7. Construct Headband

Align one short edge of the headband with the 2¾" edge of one Headband Tie, with the right sides of both fabrics facing together; and pin the two edges securely. Thread your needle, love your thread, and knot off. Stitch the two pieces together ¼" from the fabrics' raw edges, following the guidelines for felled seams on the right side on page 44, and knot off on the wrong side of the headband. Repeat this step to attach the second tie to the other side.

8. Pull Ties

Grab the headband's two ties, and pull them in opposite directions. This will cause the ties to stretch and roll into small "ropes" that you will use to tie the headband on your head.

9. Add Stretch Stitch to Headband's Long Edges

Thread your needle, love your thread, and knot off. Begin stitching on one long edge of the headband where it joins one of the ties by inserting your needle up from the bottom of the headband so that your knot is visible on the headband's wrong side. Using a zigzag chain stitch (see page 38), sew ⅛" from the cut edge across this long side, stopping when you reach the seam joining the other tie. Stitching the edge will finish it and keep it from rolling in the future after repeated washings. Repeat to finish the headband's other long side (see the illustration at right).

Add Stretch Stitch to Headband's Long Edges *(Step 9)*

Stenciling has never been merely a substitute for hand-painting but rather a utilitarian craft practiced by rich and poor alike. The ancient Chinese used stencils of the Buddha to ornament sanctuaries. The Egyptians used them to decorate their tombs. But the use of stencils reached its heyday in the early 1900s when the rise of the Arts and Crafts movement spawned books of stencil designs that people used to decorate their homes and textiles. These books offered plant and flower patterns for the kitchen, formal ornaments for living rooms, animals and bugs for family rooms, and sea life for the bathroom. I've used stencils to decorate our boxes, furniture, curtains, clay pots, and glasses, and have even made jewelry from some stencil patterns. Any of the stencils in this book can likewise be used to adorn your belongings.

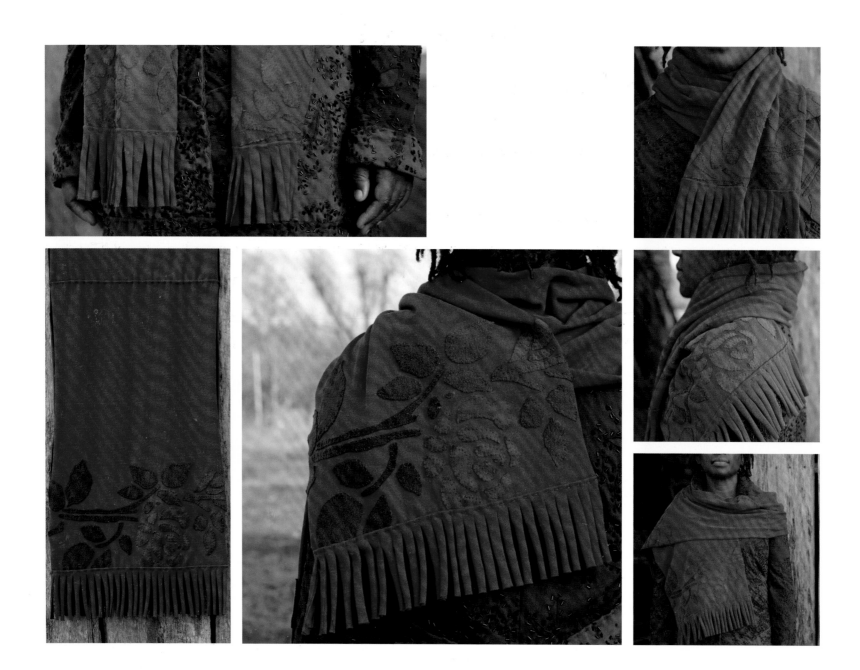

Rose Shawl

These soft cotton-jersey shawls are very popular among our clients because of their versatility. They can be worn in the winter with a heavy coat, for fall outings with a light jacket, and between seasons for a little extra warmth at night. They're also great for travel. I always carry one with me on long plane trips for comfort.

This shawl also provides a great canvas to decorate with appliqué; and, for this project, we've used the Rose stencil. At one time during the Victorian era, many small, beautifully illustrated tomes were published to decipher the language of flowers. It fascinated me to read in *The Language of Flowers*, illustrated in 1884 by Kate Greenaway, that the gift of a white rose, for example, meant "I am worthy of you"—a great basis for friendship. I once based a whole collection of garments on roses as an homage to my great-grandmother, who had a large, colorful rose garden and a passion for gardening.

My Design Choices

Top fabric	– Burgundy red
Backing fabric	– Dark burgundy red
Appliqué rose	– Light brown
Appliqué leaf and stem	– Dark brown
Paint	– Brown
Thread	– Burgundy

Supplies

Four cotton-jersey T-shirts *(two for the shawl, one for rose appliqué, and one for leaf and stem appliqués)*

14" x 22" rectangle of pattern paper *(for paper options, see page 23)*

Rose stencil *(see page 113)*

Garment scissors

Embroidery scissors

Tailor's chalk or disappearing-ink fabric pen

Tools for your choice of stencil-transfer method *(see page 28)*

Pins

Needle

Buttonhole, carpet, and craft thread

Shawl Piece Pattern *(Step 1)*

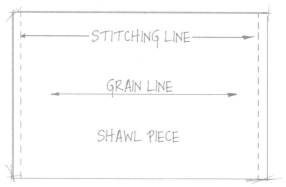

1. Make Pattern

On your 14" x 22" rectangle of pattern paper, draw a line parallel to one long side and label the line "Grain Line" and the entire pattern piece "Shawl Piece."

2. Deconstruct T-Shirts

Deconstruct the four T-shirts (see page 48), so you have a sleeveless tube of fabric that's separated at the shoulder seams. Cut each fabric tube into separate front and back panels by cutting from the bottom edge below the center of one armhole straight up to that center armhole and then repeating the process on the other side of the tube.

3. Cut Out Shawl Pattern Piece

Lay the Shawl Piece pattern on top of the T-shirt fabric you want to use for the shawl's top, making sure the pattern's marked grain line and the fabric's grain line (see page 48) run in the

same direction. With tailor's chalk, carefully trace around the pattern piece; remove the pattern; then cut out the piece, making sure to cut just inside the chalked line to remove it entirely. Repeat this step two more times, so you have three shawl pieces; you will stitch these three pieces together to form the shawl's top.

Lay out the T-shirt fabric designated for the shawl's backing layer, with the fabric's right side up; and place one cut Shawl Piece on it, making sure the grain lines of the two fabrics run in the same direction. Carefully cut around the edge of the top piece so that you have a duplicate backing piece. (Using the cut fabric pattern piece as the pattern rather than the paper pattern piece automatically adds $1/16$" extra on the piece you're cutting—exactly the extra amount we like to add to a backing piece to get the best results with appliqué.) Repeat this step two more times for a total of three backing pieces.

4. Transfer Rose Stencil Design

Prepare Rose stencil from page 113, following the directions on page 58, and enlarging the stencil by 200 percent. For this shawl, we appliquéd its two ends and left the middle section plain. Lay out two of the Shawl Pieces you cut, then use your choice of stencil-transfer method to transfer the Rose stencil on the opposite ends of the two pieces, as shown below.

5. Making Appliqué Pieces

After transferring your stencils to the ends of the shawl top, count how many roses, leaves, and stems you have, so you'll know how many appliqué pieces to make in each color to sew over your stenciled design. To create these appliqué pieces, you'll first need to transfer the stencil design to the wrong side of your appliqué fabric (the marker or paint you use to transfer the design [see page 28] will be hidden once you cut out the appliqués and turn them right side up to sew onto the shawl). To transfer the design, flip the stencil over to its wrong side, and lay out your appliqué fabrics wrong side up. (If you used paint to transfer your design in Step 4, let the stencil dry completely before flipping it over and transferring the design.)

Start by transferring all the roses from the stencil to the wrong side of the appliqué fabric you designated for the roses. Next transfer all the leaves and stems to the back of the fabric designated for these appliqués. After transferring all the design's elements, carefully cut around each stenciled area right on the edge of the transferred design.

6. Stitch Appliqué

Prepare for appliquéing by aligning and pinning the two shawl-top stenciled layers to their duplicate backing layers. Then pin your first appliqué, right side up, on top of stenciled shape it matches. Thread your needle, "love" your thread (see page 21), and knot off (see page 40). Insert your needle from the wrong side of the shawl into the backing layer and up through the shawl top, and the appliqué $\frac{1}{8}$" from the appliqué's cut edge. Using the whipstitch (see page 39), which is easy, secures the appliqué well, and looks great, stitch around the shape, making your stitches about $\frac{1}{8}$" apart. Knot off on the wrong side once you get back to your beginning knot. Move on to the next stenciled shape, pin your appliqué over it, and whipstitch around its perimeter. Continue stitching, following the guidelines for appliqué on page 62, until you've attached all the appliqués in your design.

Transfer Rose Stencil Design *(Step 4)*

7. Construct Shawl

Lay the unstenciled middle section of the shawl top on top of its duplicate backing layer, and align the edges of the two layers. Then align and pin each of the shawl's end sections to the middle section, with the right sides of the fabric facing together. Thread your needle, love your thread, and knot off. Using a straight stitch (see page 36), start stitching each seam $1/4$" from the fabrics' cut edges, beginning and ending the seam by wrap-stitching (see page 45) its edges to keep it from pulling later with wear. "Fell" the seam allowance to one side (see page 44), and stitch the allowance down using a straight stitch, beginning and ending the seam with a wrap-stitch.

8. Make Fringe

Cut four 4" x 14" rectangles from the T-shirt scraps that you used for the shawl's top layer. Stitch two rectangles as a unit to each end of shawl, with right sides together, so the seam allowances sit on the shawl's wrong side. Fell the seam allowances towards what will become the fringe, using a straight stitch and beginning and ending with wrap-stitches to secure these felled seams. Use your garment scissors to cut fringe in these shawl ends, slashing the fabric to $1/8$" from the seam line every $1/2$".

Making Your Own Label

When you finish a project, we think you should credit your efforts and celebrate your work by taking time to sign and date it. At the beginning of Alabama Chanin, we rubber-stamped our labels onto pieces of scrap jersey using a stamp and inkpad from a local office-supply store; then we sewed them to the inside back of our garments. This is a very inexpensive technique, and eventually the ink washes away; but I have a fondness for this method because it's so easy and straightforward. Stationery stores will custom-make a rubber stamp with your signature or any other graphic you like, and there are also great online sources for stamps. You can also write directly on the fabric with a Sharpie marker, or simply embroider a piece of fabric and stitch it on your garment. Another easy solution: Buy iron-on labels, and write a personal message freehand to create a customized label. Once you become more prolific, you may want to "professionalize" your label design with your own logo and get it manufactured by a printed- or woven-label company.

However you choose to sign your work, remember that the pieces you make will mark the passing of time with the love and passion that you pass on to each and every stitch.

Construct Shawl *(Step 7)*

SEAM LINE — FELLED STITCHING LINE

Rose Stencil

Note: For projects in this book, the Rose stencil was enlarged by 200 percent.

Reverse-Appliqué Book Cover

There's nothing I love more than sitting down to read a book—cookbooks, vintage crafting and sewing books, children's books, novels, art books, memoirs, and just about anything else that has pages bound together.

There are books I keep beside my bed to look at over and over again, like those about gardening or cooking. There are paperback novels with cracked spines that I've read more than a dozen times. And I also have a library in my home where books are catalogued, so I can easily find one when I need it for reference or to share with a friend or colleague.

I first made this book cover to protect an old art book whose cover had worn thin from years of use. You can make similar covers to protect and personalize journals, like those I've kept on and off since I was fifteen years old. You can even turn a simple three-ring binder into a beautiful object that can be used for years and years.

My Design Choices | Top layer   - Burgundy
Backing layer - Sage
Thread   - Sage

Supplies

Book to be covered

Two cotton-jersey T-shirts in different colors

Two pieces of pattern paper, one piece large enough to wrap around book with 1" border and second piece about 4" wide and same height as book *(for different paper options, see page 23)*

Bloomers stencil *(see pullout after page 144)*

Pencil

Transparent ruler

Tailor's chalk

Sharpie marker or your choice of tool for stencil-transfer *(see page 28)*

Garment scissors

Embroidery scissors

Pins

Needle

Buttonhole, carpet, and craft thread

1. Make Pattern

Open the book you're covering, with its spine down, on a piece of pattern paper, making sure the book is lying completely flat. Using a pencil and the transparent ruler, trace a straight line around each edge of the book. Use the ruler to add a 1/4" seam allowance on the top and bottom of your rectangle (see illustration below).

To provide for a book flap on each end of the cover, measure one-third of the book's total open width, and add this measurement to each end of your traced rectangle. For example, if your book measures 12" open, add 4" to each side for your flaps. Cut out the rectangle, and label the grain line as shown in the illustration below. This becomes your Book Cover Pattern.

Make Book-Cover Pattern *(Step 1)*

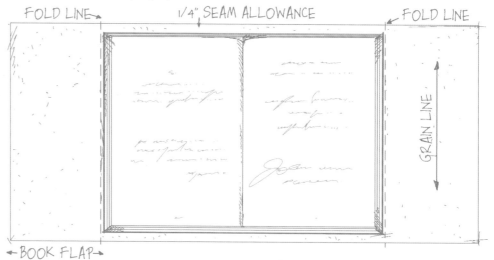

2. Prepare for Cutting

Deconstruct the two T-shirts (see page 48), so you have a sleeveless tube of fabric that's separated at the shoulder seams. Cut each tube of fabric from the bottom edge below the center of one armhole straight up to that center armhole, so the shirt opens out to lie flat as a single layer.

3. Cut Out Two Book-Cover Pieces

Decide which T-shirt you want to use for the top layer (outside) of your book cover, and lay your Book Cover Pattern on top of it, making sure your pattern's marked grain line runs in the same direction as the T-shirt fabric's grain line (see page 48). With tailor's chalk, trace around your pattern's edges, remove the pattern, and cut just inside the chalked line to remove it entirely.

Lay the cut top layer directly on top of the second, opened-out T-shirt, making sure the grain lines of both fabrics run in the same direction. Cut around the outside edge of the top layer to cut the backing layer. (Using the cut fabric piece as a pattern rather than the paper pattern automatically adds 1/16" to the backing fabric piece — exactly the extra amount of fabric that we like to add to a backing piece.)

4. Stencil Design on Top Layer of Book Cover

Lay the book cover's top layer with the right side facing up (see page 48). Place the Bloomers stencil on the top layer, and use the Sharpie marker to carefully trace the stencil onto this layer. Once you've traced the stencil, move it to any area of the top layer not covered by the stenciled design, and trace the stencil in its new position. Make sure that the stenciled design covers the entire top layer and extends to the edges of your fabric.

5. Pin Top and Backing Layers Together

Center the top layer of the book cover with the stenciled design over the book-cover backing layer, with the right sides of both pieces facing up. Using the patting method (see page 52), smooth the two pieces into place and align their edges, so they sit directly on top of one another. Securely pin the top and backing layers together.

6. Stitch Around Shapes in Stenciled Design

Thread your needle, "love" your thread (see page 21), and knot off (see page 40). Begin stitching around one of the stenciled shapes on your book cover by inserting your needle down through the cover's top layer, so your knot shows on the cover's right side. Bring your needle back up to the top layer, and, using a straight stitch (see page 36), sew around the shape until you reach your starting knot. Knot off on the top of the cover; then move on to stitch around the next shape. Continue stitching around each appliqué shape, following the guidelines for reverse appliqué on page 64.

7. Cut Reverse Appliqué

Following the instructions for reverse appliqué, carefully separate the two layers on one of the appliquéd shapes, and use your embroidery scissors to make a small slit through the top layer only of the shape. Then insert your embroidery scissors into the clipped hole, and trim away the entire top layer of the shape's interior, stopping $\frac{1}{8}$" from your stitching line. Repeat the trimming process with each reverse-appliquéd shape.

8. Construct Cover

Place your book cover face down on the table, and fold in the book flap on each end, aligning the raw edges (see bottom right). Pin the folded edges securely into place.

Using a straight stitch, join these flaps to the outside book cover, making sure to stitch $\frac{1}{4}$" from the edges across both the top and bottom edges of the flaps. Insert book.

Construct Cover *(Step 8)*

FOLD AND STITCH FLAPS CLOSED.

PAPER COVERS

When I'm working on an important presentation, I stencil and stitch the cover, so it will make a strong impression. This same technique can be used for scrapbooks, photo albums, or any other kind of bound book you might want to make.

Supplies

8½" x 11" piece of card stock or poster board-type paper

Stencil

Textile paint or tools for your choice of stencil-transfer method *(see page 28)*

T-pin

Scrap of Foam core or corrugated cardboard

Needle

Buttonhole, carpet, and craft thread

1"- to 2"-wide strip of cotton jersey for tie (optional)

1. Transfer the stencil to your 8½" x 11" piece of card stock, using your choice of stencil-transfer method. Before moving to Step 2, let the card stock dry if you used paint.

2. Place the dried card stock on top of the foam core or corrugated cardboard.

3. Using the T-pin, punch holes at ¼" intervals along the edge of the transferred design. These holes will serve as your stitching guide.

4. Thread the needle, "love" your thread (see page 21), and tie off the thread using a double knot (see page 40).

5. Stitch around each stenciled shape, knotting off when you reach your starting point.

6. Grab one end of cotton strip in each hand and pull to make strip roll on itself. Tie around book to bind.

Rose & Lace Stripe Shirt

Some of you may laugh at this, but I never really understood the saying "A stitch in time saves nine." And after asking many of my contemporaries, it seemed that no one else knew what it meant either! But I learned the meaning when I noticed a small hole in a favorite T-shirt. I knew that I should fix it, but I just never got around to it. After washing that shirt a few times, the hole got bigger and bigger. So, here's the lesson: If you start to get a hole in something, you should fix it immediately. If you wait until later, the hole will get bigger; and you'll need a lot more stitches (and time or money) to fix it. This saying seems to apply to most problems in life—the longer you leave them unattended, the harder they are to solve.

This project, which combines appliqué and reverse appliqué, is excellent for salvaging favorite T-shirts with holes (or even small stains). You can also adapt it in order to recycle other pieces in your wardrobe.

My Design Choices

T-shirt	– Light blue
Backing fabric	– Cream
Appliqué fabric	– Light brown
Thread	– Cream for reverse appliqué, tan for appliqué
Knots	– Positioned on shirt's wrong side

Supplies

One short-sleeve cotton-jersey T-shirt in your size

Two cotton-jersey T-shirts in different colors
(or cotton-jersey scraps)

Lace Stripe stencil *(see page 78)*

Rose stencil *(see page 113)*

Garment scissors

Embroidery scissors

Tailor's chalk or disappearing-ink fabric pen

Tools for your choice of stencil-transfer method *(see page 28)*

Pins

Needle

Buttonhole, carpet, and craft thread

1. Prepare Stencils

Photocopy the Lace Stripe stencil, enlarging it by 300 percent. Photocopy the Rose stencil, enlarging it by 200 percent. Prepare and cut the stencils according to the instructions on page 58.

2. Stencil Lace Stripe on T-Shirt

Place the T-shirt that you're using as a base on your work surface, making sure that the T-shirt's front faces up. Place the Lace Stripe stencil over your T-shirt; and, using your choice of stencil-transfer method, carefully transfer the stencil design to the T-shirt. Then reposition the stencil and transfer the design again as needed so that it extends from the T-shirt's bottom edge up to the shoulder seam. If you used paint to transfer the stencil, let the paint dry on both the fabric and the stencil before moving on to Step 3.

Stencil Rose Design on T-Shirt *(Step 3)*

3. Stencil Rose Design on T-Shirt

Place the Rose stencil on your T-shirt, as shown in the illustration at left (note that you'll be stenciling over the Lace Stripe stenciled in Step 2). Using your choice of stencil-transfer method, carefully transfer the stencil onto the T-shirt. Set aside the Rose stencil to dry, so you can use it again in Step 5.

4. Deconstruct the Two T-shirts

Deconstruct your two additional T-shirts, as explained on page 48, so that you have a sleeveless tube of fabric that's separated at the shoulder seams. Cut each tube of fabric into separate front and back panels by cutting from the bottom edge below the center of one armhole straight up to that center armhole and then repeating the process on the other side.

5. Make the Appliqué Pieces

Using the wrong side of the Rose stencil and following the instructions for appliqué on page 62, transfer the Rose stencil onto the wrong side of one of your deconstructed T-shirt fabrics. (Since you're stenciling on the appliqué fabric's wrong side, the marker or paint you use for transferring the stencil won't show when you turn the appliqué pieces right side up to attach them.)

6. Add Reverse-Appliqué Fabric

Cut a piece of cotton jersey from one of your extra deconstructed T-shirts or from your fabric scraps that's about 5" x 25", or as wide and long as your Lace Stripe stencil. Carefully pin this fabric rectangle on the wrong side of your base T-shirt behind the stenciled Lace Stripe design. As you position the two fabrics, make sure the grain lines on both fabrics run in the same direction (see page 48) and that the scrap fabric's right side faces the T-shirt's wrong side (inside).

7. Stitch Reverse Appliqué

Thread your needle, "love" your thread (see page 21), and knot off (see page 40). Begin stitching one of the Lace Stripe designs, by inserting your needle up through the wrong side of your T-shirt through the backing fabric, so the knot sits on the shirt's wrong side. Using a straight stitch (see page 36), sew around one of the shapes in your stenciled design, stitching right on the shape's edge. When you arrive back at your starting point, knot off thread on the T-shirt's wrong side; then move on to stitch around the next shape. Continue stitching around the remaining stenciled shapes, following the guidelines for reverse appliqué on page 64.

8. Trim Top Layer of Reverse Appliqué

Following the instructions for reverse appliqué, separate the two layers on one of the reverse appliqué shapes, and clip through the top layer only with your embroidery scissors. Insert your scissors into this clipped hole, and trim away the entire interior of the shape, stopping $\frac{1}{8}$" from the stitching line. Continue clipping and trimming the top layer of all the shapes in your stenciled image.

9. Stitch Appliqué Pieces

Carefully cut around each appliqué piece of the Rose that you stenciled in Step 3. Working on the right side of the base T-shirt and with the Rose appliqué's right side up, pin the appliqués to the transferred Rose design on the T-shirt. Thread your needle, love your thread, and knot off. Insert your needle from the wrong side of your T-shirt up through one of the Rose appliqué pieces, and whipstitch (see page 39) around the entire shape. Knot off your thread on the wrong side of the T-shirt, and move on to the next shape to stitch around it in the same way. Continue stitching around all the remaining shapes, following the guidelines for appliqué.

Rooster & Rose Tablecloth

Every spring the staff at Alabama Chanin hosts a community picnic. Friends and family from near and far come to enjoy our little corner of the world. We sit under tents, listen to music, catch up on each other's tales, and eat an enormous potluck feast with a bounty of down-home cooking.

I love setting the tables on picnic morning and usually add clay pots and tin cans filled with newly sprouting vegetables and spices that will be planted in the garden a few weeks later. Putting out tablecloths like this one and getting the napkins ready are signs that winter is over and that we'll soon be enjoying home-grown flowers, fruits, and vegetables.

My Design Choices

Tablecloth fabric – Cream
Backing fabric   – Royal blue
Appliqué Fabric   – Royal blue
Paint   – Grey
Thread   – Cream
Knots   – Positioned on wrong side of tablecloth

Supplies

3 yards of cotton-jersey fabric at least 60" wide, or buy tubular cotton-jersey fabric and slit open

Four cotton-jersey T-shirts

Rooster stencil *(see page 88)*

Rose stencil *(see page 113)*

Garment scissors

Embroidery scissors

Tailor's chalk or disappearing-ink fabric pen

Tools for your choice of stencil-transfer method *(see page 28)*

Yardstick or measuring tape

Pins

Needle

Buttonhole, carpet, and craft thread

1. Prepare Tablecloth Base

Using your yardstick or measuring tape, measure and cut the cotton-jersey yardage 84" long x 60" wide. Before cutting, make sure that your fabric's grain line (see page 48) runs parallel with what will be the tablecloth's 84" side.

2. Prepare Stencils

Photocopy the Rooster stencil, enlarging it by 455 percent. Photocopy the Rose stencil, enlarging it by 200 percent. Prepare and cut the stencils according to the instructions on page 58.

3. Stencil Designs on Tablecloth

Lay your tablecloth fabric right side up (see page 48). Place the Rooster stencil in the middle of one long edge of the tablecloth, as shown below. Using your choice of stencil-transfer method, transfer the stencil (see page 58). Repeat, transferring the stencil

Prepare Tablecloth Base *(Step 1)*

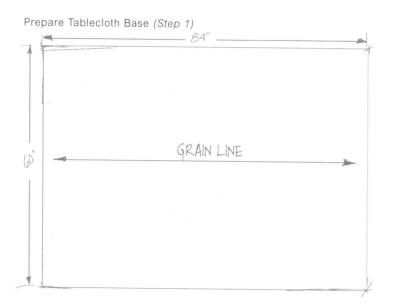

Stencil Designs on Tablecloth *(Step 3)*

in the center of the opposite edge of the tablecloth. With the tablecloth still lying face up, position your Rose stencil on one side of the transferred Rooster stencil, and carefully transfer the stencil. Repeat in alternating directions on either side of the Rooster until you've completed the edge. Then repeat the process on the opposite edge.

4. Cut Backing Fabric for Rose's Stems and Leaves

Deconstruct the T-shirts as explained on page 48, and cut eight rectangles from the T-shirt fabric that are each large enough to be placed behind one transferred Rose stencil. (Before cutting the backing-fabric sections, make sure that the cut fabric's grain line will run in the same direction as the tablecloth's grain line.) Position and pin each cut backing-fabric rectangle, so its right side faces the tablecloth's wrong side.

5. Stitch Rose's Leaves and Stems for Reverse Appliqué

Thread your needle, "love" your thread (see page 21), and knot off (see page 40). Using a straight stitch (see page 36), begin stitching one of the leaves or stems on a stenciled rose, bringing the needle up from the tabelcloth's wrong side through the backing fabric. When you return to where you began stitching, knot off your thread on the tablecloth's wrong side. Knot your thread anew, and start stitching around the next leaf or stem, as before. Repeat this process to stitch around all the leaves and stems.

6. Trim Interior Shapes on Reverse Appliqué

Follow the instructions for trimming the top layer of fabric on the interior of these shapes, as explained on page 65.

7. Appliqué Rose Stencil

Deconstruct the T-shirt you want to use for the Rose appliqué. Turn the Rose stencil to the wrong side, and position it on the wrong side of the appliqué fabric (be sure the stencil is dry from the previous transfer). Using your choice of stencil-transfer method, transfer the stencil and let it dry. Repeat the stencil-transfer process seven more times to make eight Rose appliqués. Cut out the appliqués' individual petals.

8. Stitch Appliqués

Align and pin each Rose petal appliqué, with the appliqué fabric's right side up, to a matching stenciled petal on the tablecloth. Thread your needle, love your thread, and knot off; insert the needle from the tablecloth's wrong side, and bring it up to the top through the edge of one appliqué petal. Using a whipstitch (see page 39), sew around the petal's edge. Knot off on the fabric's wrong side when you arrive back where you started. Rethread your needle, and whipstitch around the next petal, continuing this way to stitch around all the appliqués.

9. Appliqué Rooster

Repeat steps 4 through 8, using your Rooster stencil to create and attach a Rooster appliqué to the center of each edge of your tablecloth. We appliquéd all of the Rooster's feathers, and the feet, and reverse-appliquéd the body.

Rag Boa

Boas can have the sass of Mae West or the sophistication of an Edwardian lady. This Rag Boa is my own version of the classic feather variety. It can take on many characters depending on the choice of color, making it a great way to experiment with color combinations you may have never considered before.

Because you can use unwanted and damaged T-shirts or other cotton-jersey scraps for this project, it's a fun way to transform what you already have into something inspiring and new. And if you're like my friend Eva Whitechapel, you'll discover that this boa is fun and practical. She whips hers off occasionally to do a little dusting!

My Design Choices | T-shirt #1 - Cream and red stripe
T-shirt #2 - Brown
Thread   - Red

Supplies

Two cotton-jersey T-shirts or cotton-jersey scraps in two different colors

Three pieces of pattern paper, one 9" x 23", one 7" x 23", and one 5" x 23" *(for different paper options, see page 23)*

Garment scissors

Embroidery scissors

Measuring tape or yardstick

Tailor's chalk or disappearing-ink fabric pen

Pins

Needle

Buttonhole, carpet, and craft thread

1. Make Pattern

On your 9" x 23" piece of pattern paper, draw a line parallel to one long side, and label the line "Grain Line" and the rectangle itself "Boa Center."

Repeat this process with your 7" x 23" piece of pattern paper, labeling the line you add "Grain Line" and this rectangle "Boa Middle."

Repeat this process with your 5" x 23" piece of pattern paper, labeling the line you add "Grain Line" and this rectangle "Boa Outside."

2. Prepare Fabric for Cutting

Deconstruct your two T-shirts as explained on page 48 so that you have a sleeveless tube of fabric that's separated at the shoulder seams. Then cut each T-shirt tube from the bottom edge below the center of one armhole straight up to that center armhole, so the tube can open out flat as a single layer.

3. Cut Boa Center and Outside Pieces

Place your Boa Center pattern on top of the deconstructed T-shirt you want to use for the boa's middle, or center, layer, making sure the pattern's marked grain line and the T-shirt's grain line (see page 48) run in the same direction. With tailor's chalk, trace around your pattern's edges, remove the pattern, and cut out your Boa Center, cutting just inside the chalked line to remove it entirely. Repeat the process to cut two more Boa Centers from this fabric.

Working with the same T-shirt fabric, repeat this process, using the pattern for the Boa Outside; and cut six Boa Outside pieces.

4. Cut Boa Middle Pieces

Place your Boa Middle pattern on top of your second deconstructed T-shirt, making sure that the pattern's marked grain line and the T-shirt's grain line run in the same direction. With tailor's chalk, trace around your pattern's edges, remove the pattern, and cut out six Boa Middles, cutting just inside the chalked line to remove it entirely.

5. Assemble Boa Center

Place one Boa Center piece on your work surface, and overlap by 1" one end of that piece with a second Boa Center piece. Repeat at the opposite end with the third Boa Center, so the three Boa Centers make up one "continuous" 67" x 9" strip of cotton jersey (see the illustration at top right).

Assemble Boa Center, Middle, and Outside *(Step 5 and 6)*

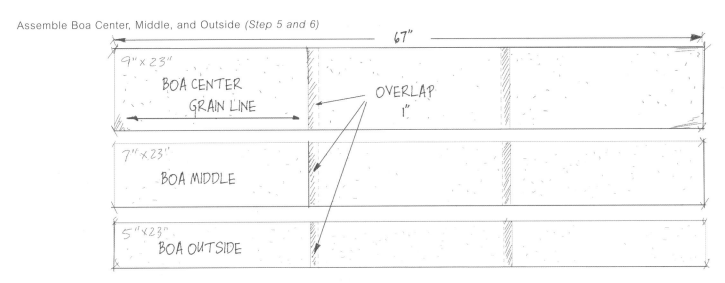

67"

9" x 23"
BOA CENTER
GRAIN LINE

OVERLAP
1"

7" x 23"
BOA MIDDLE

5" x 23"
BOA OUTSIDE

6. Add Boa Middle and Boa Outside

Repeat the above process, layering three Boa Middles on top of the Boa Centers, and then layering three Boa Outsides on top of the Boa Middles, staggering the positioning of the overlapping edges slightly on each different layer (see the illustration below).

Pin the layered pieces securely, and turn the unit over to the other side. Repeat the layering process, adding and pinning as before, the Boa Middle and Outside pieces to the unit (see the cross-section illustration below of the layered boa ready for stitching).

Add Boa Middle and Boa Outside *(Step 6)*

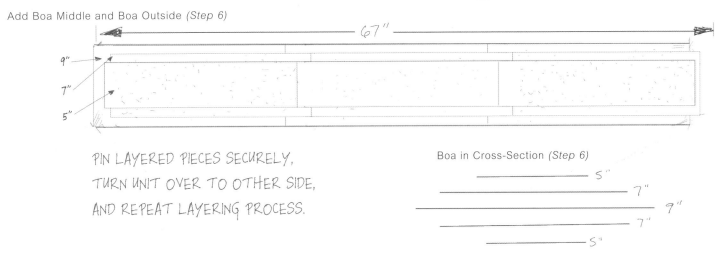

67"

9"
7"
5"

PIN LAYERED PIECES SECURELY,
TURN UNIT OVER TO OTHER SIDE,
AND REPEAT LAYERING PROCESS.

Boa in Cross-Section *(Step 6)*

5"
7"
9"
7"
5"

7. Stitch Boa

Thread your needle, "love" your thread (see page 21), and knot off (see page 40). Begin stitching down the middle of one of the Boa Outsides, inserting your needle down through all the layers. Bring your needle back up to the top; and, using a straight stitch (see page 36), stitch straight down the center of the five layers. Knot off after stitching to the opposite end of the boa.

8. Cut Fringe

Using your garment scissors, make a series of parallel cuts ½" apart on one long edge of the boa through all five layers, stopping ½" from your stitching line. Repeat this process on the opposite long edge.

9. Separate Fringe

Working outdoors or over an old sheet, shake your finished boa vigorously to separate the individual strands of fringe and remove the excess fibers the cutting process produced.

Stitch Boa *(Step 7)*

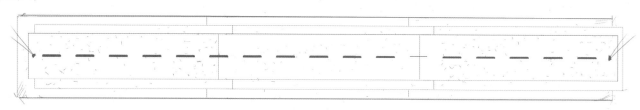

Cut Fringe *(Step 8)*

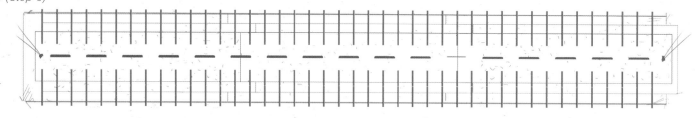

CUT THROUGH ALL LAYERS ON EACH SIDE, ½" APART AND STOPPING ½" FROM STITCHING LINE.

Flower Bouquet

I'm an avid gardener. There's hardly anything I find more satisfying than digging my hands into the dirt, planting seeds, and watching them grow. But it's sometimes difficult to find time to spend in the garden. I think that's why so many of our Alabama Chanin collections are inspired by flowers—like climbing daisies, clematis, and roses.

Of course, flowers are known for their natural beauty and scent, but when freshly cut ones are unavailable, this cotton-jersey variety made from scraps of T-shirt fabric is a great substitute. There's an old wives' tale about changing the spirit of your home by simply adding flowers—and I believe it's true.

My Design Choices

Fabric for flowers – White, cream, light pink, and dark pink
Fabric for leaves – Moss green
Thread – Cream
Floral wire – Bark-covered wire

Supplies

Four cotton-jersey T-shirts in different colors or scraps of cotton-jersey fabric, each at least 1½" x 20" *(you'll need ten strips per mum)*

One cotton-jersey T-shirt in green *(for leaves)*

One ½" x 20" piece of pattern paper *(for different paper options, see page 23)*

24" transparent plastic ruler

Pencil

Rotary cutter and cutting mat

Iron

Garment scissors

Embroidery scissors

Tailor's chalk or disappearing-ink fabric pen

Pins

Needle

Buttonhole, carpet, and craft thread

Floral wire

1. Cut Mum Strips

We created six large mums for our bouquet, with each large mum made up of five small mums. For each small mum, you'll need two cut strips of cotton jersey (see the dimensions at right), or a total of the sixty strips to make six large mums.

Using your garment scissors, cut sixty strips of cotton jersey in different colors, each 1½" x 20". Switching to your embroidery scissors, cut slits about ¼" apart along each strip, stopping ½" from the bottom edge (see the top illustration on the facing page).

2. Roll Pair of Mum Strips and Stitch

Select two of the fabric strips you cut in Step 1, align their edges, and roll them together along their uncut edge (see the illustration at the bottom left on the facing page).

Thread your needle, "love" your thread (see page 21), and knot off (see page 40). Secure the uncut, rolled bottom edges of the two strips making up a small mum by stitching through all layers several times to join them. Repeat the process to create four more small mums.

3. Make Floral-Wire Stems

Make a stem for each large mum by cutting a piece of floral wire to your desired length and twisting a loop in one end of the wire by rolling the wire around your finger.

4. Attach Small Mums to Stems

Attach the five small mums to each stem by sewing them through and around the stem's loop.

5. Cut Flat Leaves

Fold the green cotton-jersey fabric in half. Using your garment scissors and the Flat Leaf pattern at the bottom right of the facing page, cut out the leaf pattern to get two flat leaves to make one finished leaf. Repeat to make additional leaves for each mum.

Cut Mum Strips *(Step 1)*

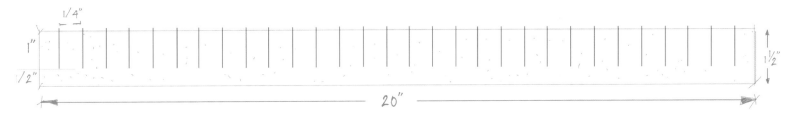

1/4"

1"

1/2"

1½"

20"

CUT SLITS 1" LONG AND 1/4" APART, LEAVE BOTTOM 1/2" UNCUT.

6. Stitch Flat Leaves

Align each pair of cut flat leaves, with the wrong sides of the fabric together, and pin them in place. Thread your needle, love your thread, and stitch around the leaf ¼" away from the cut edges, using a straight stitch (see page 36) to join the two layers.

7. Attach Leaves to Each Mum

Sew one or two finished flat leaves to each completed mum where the stem and flower meet.

Roll Pair of Mum Strips *(Step 2)*

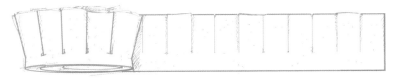

ROLL TWO CUT STRIPS TOGETHER, KEEPING UNCUT
BOTTOM EDGES ALIGNED.

Flat Leaf Pattern *(Step 5)*

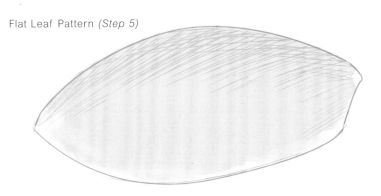

Over-the-Arm Pincushion

The design for this over-the-arm pincushion is based on one that was passed down to me by my grandmother. Hers came from a long-ago church bazaar; its maker has always been a mystery to us. One day while I was using it, I found a clue, albeit a vague one. Folded up on a piece of lined paper deep inside was this simple poem written in neat script: "I'm an Arm Chair Caddy, a very handy tool you'll see. Put your thread and scissors in my pocket, pins and needles in the middle of me. When you are finished sewing, fold me up as I am. Put me away 'til next time you need a helping hand."

I imagine that my grandmother discovered the poem long before I did and decided—like me—to keep it tucked away inside as a small reminder of the maker's pride.

My Design Choices

Top fabric	– Cream
Backing fabric	– Gold
Stencil-transfer method	– Fine-point Sharpie marker
Thread	– Cream
Knots	– Positioned inside pincushion

Supplies

Two cotton-jersey T-shirts in different colors

Two pieces of pattern paper, one 6" x 12½" and the other 4½" x 6" *(for paper options, see page 23)*

Bloomers stencil *(see pullout after page 144)*

Garment scissors

Embroidery scissors

Clear plastic ruler

Tailor's chalk or disappearing-ink fabric pen

Tools for your choice of stencil-transfer method *(see page 28)*

Cotton batting or cotton balls

2 cups of rice

Pins

Needle

Buttonhole, carpet, and craft thread

Prepare Pattern *(Step 1)*

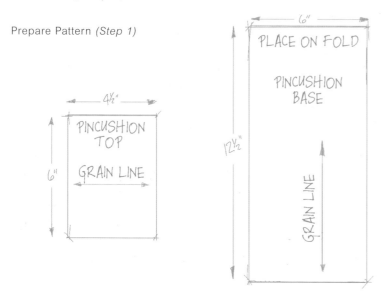

1. Prepare Pattern

On the 6" x 12½" piece of pattern paper, draw a line parallel to the 12½" side near the center of the paper, and label it "Grain Line." Then label one 6" edge with the words "Place on Fold," and label the entire pattern "Pincushion Base" (see illustration at near left).

On the 4½" x 6" piece of pattern paper, draw a line parallel to the 4½" side, and label this line "Grain Line" (see illustration at far left). Label the entire pattern "Pincushion Top."

2. Prepare Fabric

Deconstruct your two T-shirts, as explained on page 48, so that you have a sleeveless tube of fabric that's separated at the shoulder seams. Cut from the bottom left side of each tube straight up to the center of the left armhole so that the tube opens out completely as a single layer.

3. Cut Out Pattern

Lay one of your deconstructed T-shirts on a flat work surface, and fold the neckline down, so the center neckline sits on or near the bottom edge of the bottom layer. Place your Pincushion Base pattern on top of the folded T-shirt, aligning the pattern edge marked "Place on Fold" with the fold of T-shirt and making sure that the pattern's marked grain line runs in the same direction as the T-shirt's grain line (see page 48). Trace around the pattern's edges with tailor's chalk, remove the pattern, and cut out your pattern piece, cutting just inside the chalked line to remove it entirely. Repeat this step again on this T-shirt fabric. Then lay out one of the second-color panels, as before; and repeat the step twice more, so you end up with two Pincushion Base pieces in each color.

Lay your Pincushion Top pattern on a sleeve from one of your deconstructed T-shirts, and trace around the pattern's edges with tailor's chalk. Remove the pattern, and cut out your Pincushion Top, cutting just inside the chalked line to remove it entirely. Repeat the process with a sleeve in the second-color fabric, so you have one Pincushion Top in each color.

4. Stencil Design on Cut Pieces

Decide which color fabric you want to be the outer layer of your Pincushion Base, and lay the two Pincushion Base pieces in that color right side up, alongside the Pincushion Top in that color, also laid right side up. Place your Bloomers stencil over one Pincushion Base; and, using the stencil-transfer method of your choice, transfer the stencil design onto the base piece, making sure to extend the transferred design all the way to the edges of the fabric. When finished, repeat this process on the other Pincushion Base and then on the Pincushion Top.

5. Prepare Fabrics for Stitching

The Pincushion Base is composed of two duplicate layers of reverse appliqué (with each layer made of a stenciled top fabric that's stitched to a plain backing fabric and then trimmed on the interior of the stenciled shapes; see page 65 for more on reverse appliqué), which are positioned with their wrong (unstenciled) sides facing one another and their reverse-appliqué sides facing out. The Pincushion Top is a single layer of reverse appliqué that's stitched into a tube and stuffed to create the actual pincushion in the center.

To prepare each Pincushion Base layer for stitching, lay one stenciled Pincushion Base on top of an unstenciled Pincushion Base, with both fabrics right side up and their edges aligned; and pin the layers in place. Likewise, layer,

align, and pin the stenciled top fabric and unstenciled backing fabric that will make up the Pincushion Top.

6. Stitch Around Stenciled Shapes

Thread your needle, "love" your thread (see page 21), and knot off (see page 40). Begin stitching around the edge of any one of the stenciled shapes in one of your Pincushion Bases by inserting your needle up through the backing fabric to the top layer, so your knot shows on the wrong side of the Pincushion Base. After bringing your needle up to the top, straight-stitch (see page 36) around the edge of the shape, and knot off on the base's wrong side when you return to your starting place. Knot your thread again, move to a neighboring shape, and again stitch around the shape to outline it. Continue stitching and following the guidelines for reverse appliqué until you've stitched around all the stenciled shapes. Repeat the process for the second Pincushion Base layer and for the Pincushion Top.

7. Trim Reverse Appliqué

Following the instructions for reverse appliqué, carefully separate the two layers of one reverse-appliqué shape, and clip through the top layer only with your embroidery scissors. Insert your scissors into this clipped slit, and trim away the entire interior of the shape, stopping $1/8$" from your stitching line. Continue trimming the interior of all the remaining shapes.

8. Prepare Base for Construction

Place one of your Pincushion Base layers flat and face down (with its reverse-appliqué side down) on your work surface. Place the second Pincushion Base layer on top of the first one, face up (with its reverse-appliqué side up). (The wrong, un-stenciled sides of the two Pincushion Base layers will face one another.) Align all the edges of the two layers, and pin them together.

9. Stitch Base Layers Together

Thread your needle, love your thread, and knot off. Using a straight stitch, sew the pinned layers together, starting at the end of one long edge and stitching ¼" from the fabrics' raw edges. Secure the beginning and end of your seam with a wrap-stitch (see page 45). Repeat this process for the other long side of the two base layers.

10. Stitch Pockets for Rice

Measure and mark from each short edge of the Pincushion Base 6" in from that edge on both long edges. Using a straight stitch, stitch across the Pincushion Base on one end from one mark to the other to create the bottom seam of a pocket that will hold rice to weight each end of the pincushion and anchor it on the arm of a chair. Secure the beginning and end of the pocket seam by wrap-stitching its edges.

Repeat this step for other short end of Pincushion Base.

Stitch Layers and Make Pockets (*Steps 10-12*)

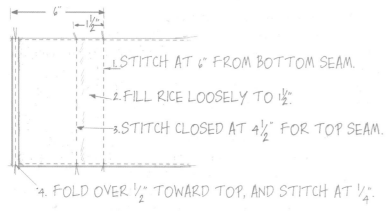

1. STITCH AT 6" FROM BOTTOM SEAM.

2. FILL RICE LOOSELY TO 1½".

3. STITCH CLOSED AT 4½" FOR TOP SEAM.

4. FOLD OVER ½" TOWARD TOP, AND STITCH AT ¼".

11. Pour in Rice and Seal Pocket

Separate the two layers on one end of the Pincushion Base, and pour rice into the pocket to fill 1½" from the pocket's bottom seam.

Measure in 4½" from the pocket's open edges, and straight-stitch across the opening to create the pocket's top seam and encase the rice (see left). Secure the beginning and end of the pocket's top seam by wrap-stitching its edges.

Repeat this step to fill and close the rice pocket at the other end of the Pincushion Base.

12. Fold and Stitch Raw Edges

Fold over the raw edges on the short ends of the Pincushion Base ½" toward what will be the pincushion's top side, and use a straight stitch to sew the folded edges ¼" from the fold. Wrap-stitch the beginning and end of the seam to secure it.

13. Fold and Stitch Tool Pockets

To make tool pockets on each short end of the Pincushion Base, fold each short end along the rice pocket's bottom seam toward what will be the pincushion's top side. Align the top and bottom edges, and pin them in place (see right).

Sew the folded pockets in place, straight-stitching along each pinned edge ¼" from the edge. Begin and end each pocket seam by wrap-stitching its edges to secure the seam.

Anatomy of the Finished Pincushion *(Step 13 -15)*

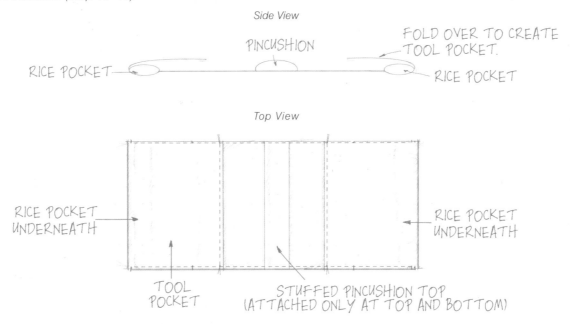

Side View

RICE POCKET

PINCUSHION

FOLD OVER TO CREATE
TOOL POCKET.

RICE POCKET

Top View

RICE POCKET
UNDERNEATH

RICE POCKET
UNDERNEATH

TOOL
POCKET

STUFFED PINCUSHION TOP
(ATTACHED ONLY AT TOP AND BOTTOM)

14. Construct the Pincushion Top

Fold the reverse-appliquéd Pincushion Top in half, with right sides together and the long edges aligned; and pin the long edges together. Thread your needle, love your thread, and knot off. Using a straight stitch and starting at one end of the pincushion's pinned long edge, sew the pinned edges together 1/4" from the fabric's raw edges. Begin and end your seam by wrap-stitching its edges to secure them. Turn the Pincushion Top right side out, so the seam is on the inside.

15. Stitch and Stuff Pincushion Top

Place your Pincushion Top in the center of the top side of your Pincushion Base, and pin its edges in place. Stitch one short end of the Pincushion Top to the Pincushion Base, using a straight stitch 1/4" from the fabric's edges, stitching through all layers, and wrap-stitching the beginning and end of the seam.

On the Pincushion Top's other short end, separate the two layers and stuff the "pocket" with cotton batting. After stuffing, straight-stitch the Pincushion Top's open edges to the Pincushion Base 1/4" from the fabric's edges, stitching through all layers, and wrap-stitching the beginning and end of the seam.

Reverse-Appliqué Corset

Corsets have been around for a very long time, and they often conjure up images of women with cinched waists, constricted by tight contraptions ribbed with whale bone and steel. Since whale bone and steel don't fit into my lifestyle, I took this classic, utterly feminine form and gave it my own modern, comfortable twist. I found that cotton jersey, constructed with strong handmade seams, provides the perfect support and at the same time allows the corset to fit any woman's body. I've heard that some of our clients call this corset "Wonder Alabama" because it shows off any woman's best assets and enhances the lovely curves that we have so naturally.

We call this piece an "allover garment" because it is entirely covered with stencil patterns. To create the allover effect, we lay out together all the cut-fabric pattern pieces for the garment's front and transfer the stencil design all at once. Then we repeat the process with the pieces making up the back of the garment. Once the pieces are sewn together, each seam line takes up about a half inch of the stenciled image, so the resulting design is slightly altered and also very contemporary and appealing.

My Design Choices

Top layer	– Dark burgundy
Backing layer	– Light burgundy
Fabric paint	– Pearl red
Thread	– Burgundy
Knots	– Positioned on corset's wrong side

Supplies

Two cotton-jersey T-shirts *(close but slightly different in color)*

Corset pattern *(see pattern sheet at back of book)*

Bloomers stencil *(see pullout after page 144)*

Garment scissors

Embroidery scissors

Rotary cutter and cutting mat

Large plastic ruler

Tailor's chalk or disappearing-ink fabric pen

Tools needed for your choice of stencil-transfer method *(see page 28)*

Needle

Pins

Buttonhole, carpet, and craft thread

All-purpose sewing thread

Iron

1. Prepare Pattern

See Step 1 of the Printed T-Shirt Corset on page 155, which uses the same pattern, for information on preparing the pattern.

2. Deconstruct T-Shirts

Deconstruct your T-shirts as explained in Step 2 of the Printed T-Shirt Corset.

3. Cut Pattern Pieces for Corset's Top and Backing Layers

Using the T-shirt panels planned for the corset's top layer, follow Steps 3 and 4 of the Printed T-Shirt Corset to cut the front and back pieces. Repeat the process with the other T-shirt panels to cut the backing-layer pieces.

4. Prepare Allover Stencil

Prepare your stencil for "allover" coverage, as explained on page 60 (and see the illustration below).

Prepare Allover Stencil *(Step 4)*

5. Stencil Design on Top Layer

Lay out the front corset's top-layer pieces, place the allover stencil over them, and transfer the stencil using your preferred transfer method (see the illustrations at right). Let the stencil dry, and repeat the process with the back corset's top-layer pieces.

6. Pin Top and Backing Layers Together

Align the top-layer and backing-layer pieces, with right sides facing up; pat the layers into place (see page 52); and pin each pair together.

Stencil Design on Top Layer *(Step 5)*

7. Baste Neck and Armhole Edges
Using a single strand of all-purpose thread, baste (see page 37) the neckline and armhole edges on each pinned pair to prevent them from stretching while you work.

8. Stitch Around Stenciled Shapes and Cut Reverse Appliqué
Stitch around all the stenciled shapes, as explained in Step 6 of the Tea Towels on page 93, and trim the top layer of the stitched shapes, as explained in Step 7.

9. Assemble Corset
Follow Steps 6 and 7 of the Printed T-Shirt Corset to assemble this corset, with one change: Sew felled seams on the right side (see page 44), not floating seams.

10. Binding Neckline and Armholes
Use the rotary cutter, cutting mat, and large plastic ruler to cut fabric strips across the grain and $1\frac{1}{4}$" wide to use as the binding for the corset's neckline and armholes. You'll need about 80" of cut strips for the binding.

Press the length of cut binding in half, wrong sides together, using your iron and being careful not to stretch the fabric while pressing it. Starting at the corset's center-back neckline, pin the folded binding around the raw edge of the corset's neckline and then overlap the binding's raw edges at the center-back about $\frac{1}{2}$", trimming any excess binding. Stitch through all layers, using a stretchable stitch (see page 38) of your choice. Repeat the process to bind each armhole.

Reverse-Appliqué Swing Skirt

This design is based on a skirt an Austrian friend made to sell in his Vienna store. I wore the skirt he gave me so frequently that, after a while, it stretched and wouldn't stay put on my hips. When I tried to get a replacement, I was disappointed to learn he no longer made this design. So, necessity being the mother of invention, I laid my old skirt on a table over pattern paper and traced around its panels to create the rough shape of the single basic pattern piece. After several markings and revisions—and more revisions and markings!—I finally had the pattern for my "dream skirt."

Over the years I've made many versions of this skirt—basic ones and heavily embroidered, beaded variations (see a beaded, appliquéd version on page 165). I've also made this skirt in a range of colors and sizes—smaller sizes for when I feel like wearing something form-fitting and larger ones for when I prefer something loose and more comfortable. Since the construction is quick and easy, it's a great basic that can be used with a variety of embellishment techniques, so it looks different every time.

My Design Choices

Top layer	– Red
Backing layer	– Brown
Fabric paint	– Burgundy red
Thread	– Brown
Knots	– Positioned on skirt's right side

Supplies

Four extra-large cotton-jersey T-shirts *(two matching for top layer and two matching for backing layer)*, or ³⁄₄ yard 60"-wide cotton jersey per color *(1¹⁄₂ yards total)*

Skirt pattern *(see pattern sheet at back of book)*

Bloomers stencil *(see pullout after page 144)*

Paper scissors

Garment scissors

Embroidery scissors

Tailor's chalk or disappearing-ink fabric pen

Tools needed for your choice of stencil-transfer method *(see page 28)*

³⁄₄ yard of 1"-wide fold-over elastic binding *(type used for diapers)*

Needle

Pins

Buttonhole, carpet, and craft thread

All-purpose sewing thread

1. Prepare Pattern

Photocopy the Swing Skirt pattern, and use paper scissors to cut the photocopied pattern to your desired size (see page 53), cutting as close as possible to the black cutting line. If you're using T-shirts instead of yardage, lay the skirt's one pattern piece on top of each of your T-shirts before cutting to make sure that the T-shirts are long enough for the pattern's length (orient the pattern vertically on the T-shirt, so the pattern's marked grain line runs in the same direction as the fabric's grain line [see page 48]). If the pattern doesn't fit, use larger T-shirts. The skirt's pattern has a ¹⁄₄" seam allowance built into its edges.

2. Deconstruct T-Shirts

If you're using yardage, go to Step 3. If you're using T-shirts, deconstruct them (see page 48), so each one is a sleeveless tube of fabric separated at the shoulder seams. Cut each tube into separate front and back panels by cutting from the bottom edge below the center of one armhole straight up to that center armhole and then repeating the process on the other side.

Prepare Pattern *(Step 1)*

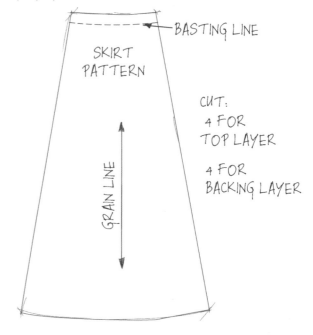

3. Cut Top-Layer Pattern Pieces

Decide which color of yardage or deconstructed T-shirts you want to use for the top layer of your skirt. Lay the skirt pattern on top of that yardage, laid flat and single layer or on top of one of the T-shirt panels, making sure the pattern's and fabric's grain lines run in the same direction. With tailor's chalk, trace around the pattern's edges, remove the pattern, and cut out the traced pattern, cutting just inside the chalked line to remove it entirely. Repeat this step with the remaining yardage or T-shirt panels in the same color to get four top layers for your skirt. (If you want, you can lay one of the deconstructed panels on top of another one, and cut out two fabric pieces at a time, but always make sure the grain lines on both fabrics run in the same direction.)

Cut Top-Layer Pattern Pieces *(Step 3)*

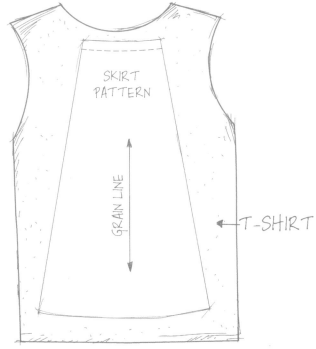

4. Cut Backing-Layer Pattern Pieces

Lay out flat and single-layer the yardage or T-shirt panels that you want to use as your backing layer, and repeat the process in Step 3 to cut four backing-layer pieces.

5. Baste Waistline

To ensure that the waistline on your cut fabric pieces doesn't stretch while you're working on your skirt, use a single strand of all-purpose thread to baste (see page 37) the waistline edges of each cut piece, as noted on the pattern piece (see the illustration on the facing page).

6. Stencil Design on Top Layer

Place one of your top-layer panels on a covered work surface, with the right side (see page 48) facing up. Lay your Bloomers stencil (or a stencil of your choice), on the panel piece. Using your preferred stencil-transfer method, transfer your stencil on the top-layer panel, moving the stencil and repeating the transfer as needed so the design extends to the fabric's edges and covers the entire panel. Repeat the stencil transfer on the remaining three top-layer panels.

7. Prepare for Stitching Panels

Center each top panel on one backing panel, with the right sides of both fabrics facing up; and pat the layers into place (see page 52) so that their edges are aligned. Securely pin the edges of both layers together.

8. Stitch Bloomers Pattern

Thread your needle, "love" your thread (see page 21), and knot off (see page 40). Begin stitching on the edge of one stenciled shape on the top panel by inserting your needle into the top panel's right side, so your knot shows on this side. After pulling the thread through on the wrong side of the backing layer, bring your needle back up to the right side of the top layer. Using a straight stitch (see page 36), start sewing around the edge of the shape. When you arrive back at your starting point, knot off your thread on the skirt's right side, then move to the next shape to stitch around it. Continue stitching around each shape in the stenciled design, following the guidelines for reverse appliqué on page 64 until you've stitched around all the shapes.

9. Cut Reverse Appliqué

Following the instructions for reverse appliqué, carefully separate the two layers, and clip through the top layer only with your embroidery scissors. Insert the scissors into this slit, and trim the entire interior of the shape, stopping $\frac{1}{8}$" from your stitching line. Continue trimming the interior of all the remaining shapes in your stencil design.

10. Prepare for Construction

Once you've stitched and trimmed the top layer of your reverse appliqué, begin constructing your skirt by pinning each pair of adjacent panels, with right sides together.

11. Construct Skirt

Thread your needle, love your thread, and knot off. Using a straight stitch, begin stitching the pinned pieces together, starting at the top edge of the skirt's waistline and stitching $\frac{1}{4}$" from the fabric's cut edges down to the bottom edge. Be sure to begin and end the seam by wrap-stitching (see page 45) its edges to secure it. "Fell" your seam by folding over the seam allowances to one side (see page 44) and topstitching the seam allowances $\frac{1}{4}$" from the cut edges (that is, down the center of the seam allowances), using a straight stitch and wrap-stitching the beginning and end of the seam.

Repeat this process to join all four panels of your skirt, making sure to check the thread tension (see page 35), so the fabric lies flat along your seam before you knot off the thread at the seam's end.

12. Add Elastic to Waistline

Fold your elastic binding in half; and, starting and ending at the center-back waistline, pin the elastic to the skirt's waistline overlapping the cut edge of the skirt's waistline, so the elastic acts as a binding and finishes that edge. Overlap the cut ends of the elastic where they meet for a clean look. We stitched the elastic binding in place with a zigzag stitch (see page 38), but any stretchable stitch will work. Thread your needle, love your thread, and knot off. Starting at the center back, where the ends of your elastic overlap, insert your needle from the skirt's wrong side, bringing it out on the right side; and zigzag-stitch all the way around the skirt to attach the elastic binding.

Note: The skirt's hem is left as a raw, unfinished edge.

TAKING CARE OF YOUR WORK

To prevent wear and tear on your garments and protect their embellishments, ideally you should hand-wash and hang-dry all your projects. But I have to admit that sometimes I throw my personal pieces in the washer and dryer. A nice compromise is to wash them in the machine in cold water on a delicate setting, hang them on a drying rack overnight, and then throw them in a hot dryer for about three minutes to dry out any remaining dampness, relax the cotton, and shrink them back into their original shape.

Embellishing with Sequins

Sequins come in a variety of sizes, shapes, luster, materials, and colors, and they make wonderful embellishments for skirts and other garments. I prefer to work with flat, matte sequins since they blend in better with our projects than shinier ones. Whatever the sequin's size or shape, we attach them in one of three ways, as you can see below. These strategies also serve as further embellishment.

Anchor Sequin with Bead On Top of It

Eyelet-Stitch Sequin in Place

Use French Knot to Anchor Sequin

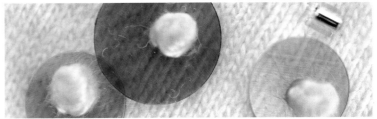

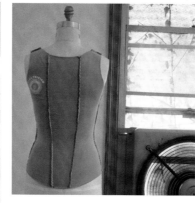

Printed T-Shirt Corset

For this project you cut up a printed T-shirt and then sew it back together so that a new graphic pattern emerges. The results never cease to surprise me. If you like, you can create two corsets at the same time by mixing and matching the pieces of two different printed T-shirts. We call these "sister shirts." Here's how to make them: Follow the instructions as given but prepare pattern pieces for two printed T-shirt corsets. Instead of using one of the T-shirts for the whole corset, mix and match by swapping out, for example, the center front panel from one of the T-shirts into the center panel of the other. Do the same with the back panels. Ultimately, you will create two shirts that are nearly alike except for the transposed panels. You'll discover how juxtaposing opposites and combining colors create a graphically pleasing result.

My Design Choices | T-shirt – Kelly green
Thread – Grey
Knots – Positioned on the corset's right side

Supplies

Cotton-jersey T-shirt with graphic print

Corset pattern *(see pattern sheet at back of book)*

Paper scissors

Garment scissors

Tailor's chalk or disappearing-ink fabric pen

Needle

Pins

Buttonhole, carpet, and craft thread

All-purpose sewing thread

1. Prepare Pattern

Photocopy the Corset pattern, and use your paper scissors to cut the photocopied pattern to your desired size (see page 53), cutting as close as possible to the black cutting line. Lay all the pattern pieces on top of your T-shirt before cutting out the pieces to make sure they all fit (orient the patterns vertically on the T-shirt, so the marked grain line on the patterns runs in the same direction as the fabric's grain line (see page 48). If the patterns don't fit, use a larger T-shirt. Every pattern piece in this garment has a $\frac{1}{4}$" seam allowance built into each edge except for the neckline, armhole, and hemline, which are left raw and unseamed for this corset.

2. Deconstruct T-Shirt

Deconstruct your T-shirt as explained on page 48 so that you have a sleeveless tube of fabric that's separated at the shoulder seams. Cut the tube into separate front and back panels by cutting from the bottom edge below the center of one armhole straight up to that center armhole and then repeating the process on the other side. Fold the front panel in half lengthwise on the shirt's grain line and exactly in the middle, so the graphic is not skewed to one side.

3. Cut Pattern Pieces for Corset Front

Place the corset's Center-Front pattern on the folded T-shirt fabric, with the pattern edge marked "Place on Fold" on the fabric's fold (see the illustration at bottom right of facing page). Next place the Middle-Front and Side-Front pattern pieces beside the Center-Front piece, with the longer Middle-Front piece in the middle. With tailor's chalk, carefully trace around the pattern pieces, remove the patterns, and cut out the front pieces, cutting just inside the chalked line to remove it entirely. You'll have five garment panels that will make up the front of your corset.

4. Cut Out Pattern Pieces for Corset Back

Fold the T-shirt's back panel in half lengthwise down the center, and place the Center-Back pattern piece on the folded fabric, positioning the edge marked "Place on Fold" on the fabric's fold. Then place the Side-Back pattern beside the Center-Back pattern, and trace around and cut out the patterns, as you did for the front of the corset. You'll have three cut pieces that will make up the back of your corset.

5. Baste Neck and Armholes

Using a single strand of all-purpose thread, baste the edges of all the necklines and armholes on the cut pieces, as labeled on the pattern pieces, to prevent them from stretching while you're working on your corset (see page 37).

6. Stitch Together Front and Back Pieces

With the wrong sides of the fabric together and the cut edges aligned, pin the two Middle-Front pieces to each side of the Center-Front piece. Following the directions for sewing floating seams on the right side on page 42 and using a straight stitch (see page 36), and the buttonhole, carpet, and craft thread, stitch the pinned pieces together $\frac{1}{4}$" from the fabric's cut edges, starting at the top edge of the corset. Wrap-stitch (see page 45)

Prepare Pattern *(Step 1)*

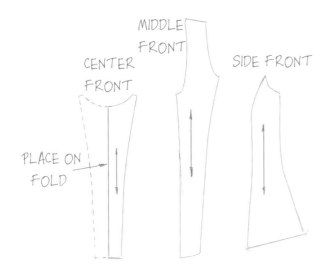

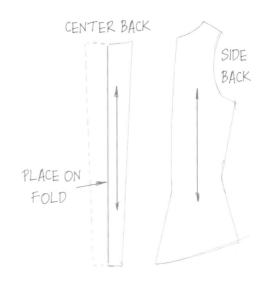

the beginning and end of each seam to secure it. As you sew, check your thread tension (see page 35), so the fabric lies flat before you knot off the thread at the seam's end.

Repeat this process to attach the Side-Front panels to the Middle-Front panels. Then repeat the process to join the three pieces of the corset's back, stitching one Side-Back panel to each side of the Center-Back panel.

7. Assemble Corset

Pin together the completed front and back panels at the shoulder seams, with the fabric's wrong sides together. Using a straight stitch, sew the shoulders together ¼" from the cut edges. Repeat this process for the side seams, sewing the wrong sides together. All seam allowances will show on corset's right side.

Cut Pattern Pieces for Corset Front *(Step 3)*

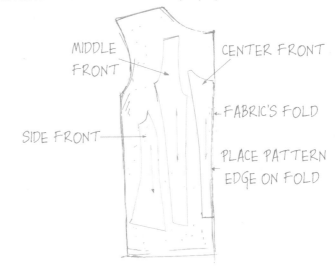

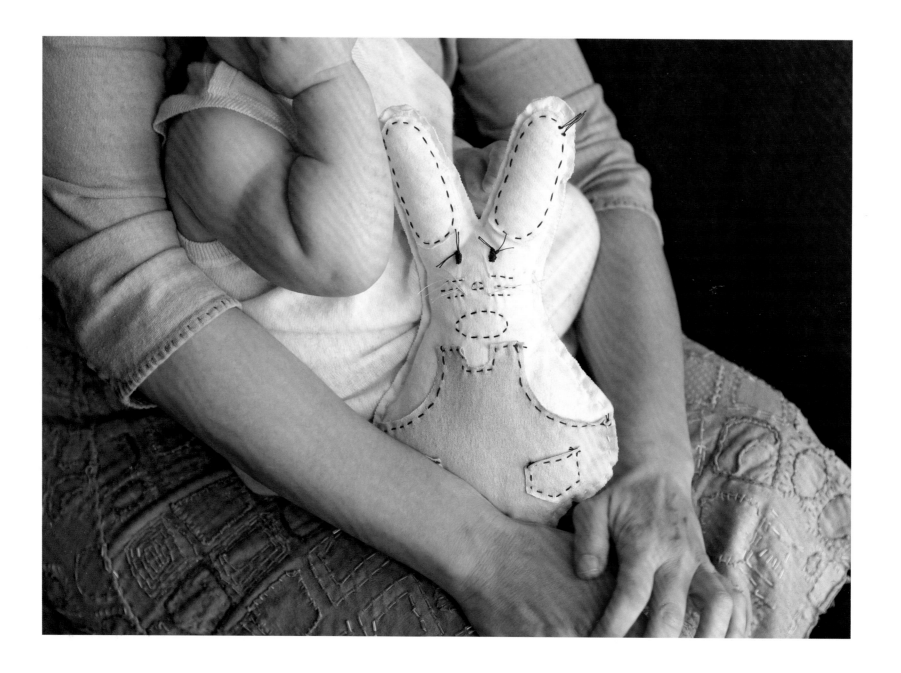

Bunny Rabbit

My grandmother used to make sock monkeys for all the children in our family. And no matter how many she made, each one of them took on its own personality and looked different from the others. This bunny rabbit is Alabama Chanin's version of the old-time favorite. It's easy to complete and, when stuffed with cotton balls or batting, can be thrown in the washer and dryer for easy cleaning. You may decide to approach it like a jack-o-lantern and design a face that expresses the mood of the moment, or ask a child to draw a face onto the fabric with a Sharpie marker or disappearing-ink pen, which you can embroider afterwards. Each time you make this project, you can be sure that your bunny will take on its own unique personality—just like my grandmother's sock monkeys.

My Design Choices | Body — White
Appliqué — Dark pink for overalls and pockets, light pink for ears and tail
Thread — Cream for construction, pink for nose and whiskers, brown for appliqué and embroidery

Supplies

Three cotton-jersey T-shirts, one white, one light pink, and one dark pink *(or cotton-jersey scraps: two white pieces, each 15" x 10"; one 6"-square light-pink piece; and one dark-pink piece, 10" x 8")*

Bunny pattern *(see below)*

Garment scissors

Embroidery scissors

Rotary cutter and cutting mat

Tailor's chalk or disappearing-ink fabric pen

Clear plastic ruler

Needle

Pins

Cotton batting, cotton balls, dried beans or rice, or any stuffing material you prefer

Buttonhole, carpet, and craft thread: cream, brown, and pink

1. Prepare Pattern

Photocopy the four pattern pieces below: the Body, Apron, Ear Appliqué, and Apron Pocket. These patterns can be enlarged or reduced as you like. For our bunny, we enlarged the patterns 325 percent.

2. Deconstruct T-Shirts

Deconstruct the T-shirts, as explained on page 48 so that you have a sleeveless tube of fabric that's separated at the shoulder seams. Cut each tube of fabric into separate front and back panels by cutting from the bottom edge below the center of one armhole straight up to that center armhole and then repeating the process on the other side.

Prepare Pattern *(Step 1)*

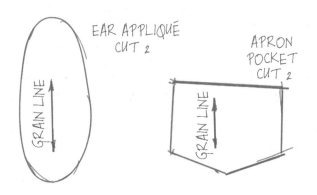

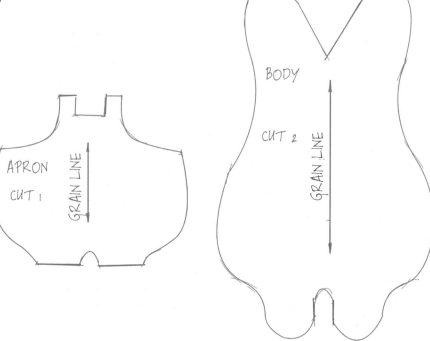

3. Cut Pattern Pieces

Lay your white deconstructed T-shirt panels on a flat work surface with wrong sides together (see page 48). Align the edges of the panels, and pat out the T-shirts, so they lie flat (see page 52). Place your bunny Body pattern on top of the fabric, matching the marked grain line on the pattern with the fabrics' grain line (see page 48). Trace around your pattern's edges with tailor's chalk, and remove the pattern. Cut out the body, cutting through both layers just inside the chalked line to remove it entirely. You'll have two body pieces: a front and a back that look exactly the same.

Lay your light-pink deconstructed T-shirt sleeves, with wrong sides together and their edges aligned, on your work surface, and pat out the sleeves, so they lie flat. Place the Ear Appliqué pattern on top of the fabric, matching the pattern's and fabric's grain line; trace around the pattern's edges with tailor's chalk, and remove the pattern. Cut out your pattern pieces, cutting through both layers just inside the chalked line. You'll have two Ear Appliqués.

Lay one panel of your dark-pink deconstructed T-shirt right side up on your working surface. Pat out your T-shirt, so it lies flat. Place the Apron pattern on top of the fabric, matching the pattern's and fabric's grain line; trace around the pattern's edges with tailor's chalk; and remove the pattern. Cut out your pattern piece, cutting just inside the chalked line. You'll have one Apron piece.

Use a sleeve from the dark-pink T-shirt to cut out your Apron Pocket patterns, folding the sleeve in half vertically and placing your pattern on the fabric's lengthwise grain line. You'll have two Apron Pockets.

4. Stitch Apron Edges

Thread your needle with brown thread, "love" your thread (see page 21), and knot off (see page 40). Secure the knot on the fabric's wrong side, and straight-stitch (see page 36) along the Apron's curved edge $\frac{1}{4}$" from the raw edge, ending on the fabric's wrong side. Begin and end your seam by wrap-stitching (see page 45) its edges.

5. Stitch Pocket Edges

Thread your needle with brown thread, love your thread, and knot off. Using a straight stitch, stitch along one Pocket's straight top edge, opposite the point. Stitch $\frac{1}{4}$" from the raw edge, beginning and ending your seam by wrap-stitching its edges. Secure the knots on the fabric's wrong side. Do not stitch the straight side and bottom edges of the Pocket, just its top edge. Repeat this step for the second Pocket.

6. Stitch Apron Pockets to Apron

Place the Pocket pieces, right side up, on the Apron. Use the clear plastic ruler to align them and separate them evenly; then pin them in place. Thread your needle with brown thread, love your thread, and knot off. Using a straight stitch, stitch from each Pocket's top edge down one side, turning at the bottom point and sewing back up the opposite side. Stitch your seam $\frac{1}{4}$" from the fabric's cut edge, and begin and end the seam by wrap-stitching its edges. Do not stitch the Pocket's top edge to the Apron (after all, a bunny rabbit needs a functional pocket!), and secure all the knots on the fabric's wrong side. Repeat this process for the other Pocket.

7. Stitch Apron to Body

Place one Body piece flat and right side up on your work surface. Lay the Apron, right side up, on top of the Body, and align the curved edges of both pieces. Fold under the Apron's two top straight edges at the "shoulders" and the straight edge along the bottom $\frac{1}{4}$", and pin these folded edges in place. Leave all the Apron's other edges raw.

Thread your needle with brown thread, love your thread, and knot off. Using a straight stitch, stitch the Apron's top edge in place $\frac{1}{4}$" from the edge, starting on one side at the bunny's "waist" and stitching across the entire top edge to the other side waist. Begin and end your seam, wrap-stitching its edges and securing your knots on the fabric's wrong side. Repeat this process for the Apron's straight bottom edge. This is now your Front Body.

8. Stitch Ears

Place the Front Body, right side up, on your work surface. Lay the cut Ear Appliqués in the center of the Body's ears, and use the clear plastic ruler to align and position them evenly. Make sure the grain line of the appliqués and Front Body run in the same direction. Once you've correctly positioned and pinned the ears in place, thread your needle with brown thread, love your thread, and knot off. Using a straight stitch, stitch one ear to the Body $\frac{1}{4}$" from raw edges, and secure the knots on the right side of the Front Body. Repeat this process to sew on the other ear.

9. Stitch Face

Place the Front Body, right side up, on your work surface. It's time to draw the bunny's face, and you can be as creative as you like. After drawing on the features with a disappearing-ink pen, we straight-stitched the mouth, nose, and whiskers; whipstitched (see page 45) the nose and eyes; and made regular double knots with long tails for eyelashes and whiskers.

10. Cut Tail Piece

Use any large scrap available (we chose light pink), a rotary cutter, and a cutting mat to cut out the bunny's tail. Lay the scrap, right side up, on the cutting mat, and rotary-cut a strip of fabric 12" long and $1\frac{1}{2}$" wide, using your clear plastic ruler as a guide.

11. Stitch Tail

Lay the tail, right side up, on your work surface. Thread your needle with cream thread, love your thread, and knot off. Straight-stitch a line down the strip's center from one end to the other. When you reach the opposite end, do not knot off the thread; instead, slide your fabric down the thread to gather it up next to your knot. Once the strip is completely gathered, knot off your thread using a double knot. With the thread still attached to the gathered strip, stitch the tail directly to the right side of remaining Body piece (now your Back Body), centering it between the bunny's legs.

12. Stitch Body Front and Back Together

Lay the Back Body and Front Body on top of one another, with wrong sides facing. Align all the outside edges, and pin them together. Thread your needle with cream thread, love your thread, and knot off. Starting in the middle of the Front Body's right edge, straight-stitch ¼" from the raw edges around the entire body, stopping 4" from where you began and securing your knots on the right side of the fabric. You'll use the 4" opening in the seam for stuffing the bunny.

13. Stuff Bunny

Pushing the stuffing material of your choice into the 4" opening on the bunny's side, fill out its shape. Insert stuffing into the tips of the ears and feet first (using a crochet hook to work the stuffing into the tips of the ears and feet may help), and then fill out the middle to the thickness you want. Thread your needle with cream thread, love your thread, and knot off. Straight-stitch ¼" from the raw edges to close the opening. Secure the knots on the fabric's right side.

Threads, Flosses, Yarns, Ribbons

Over the years, I've experimented with a variety of threads, flosses, yarns, and ribbons. Each kind has its own characteristics and times when its use is appropriate. Below is a list of what my years of experience have taught me.

All-purpose thread   Good for basting.

Buttonhole, carpet, and craft thread   Use this thread doubled for hand-sewing and construction, and in all areas that are subject to real stress or wear. Available at most fabric stores as well as from many online sources, this thread can also be used as a single thread for sewing on beads and appliqué.

Embroidery floss   Appropriate for all embroidery and appliqué work, embroidery floss comes in a large variety of colors and is readily available at most fabric and craft stores. Never use this floss for seams or areas subject to stress since the strands do not wear well under stress.

Cotton yarns   Great for embroidery work where you want a heavier look. Available from some craft stores and easy to find at your local yarn shop.

Cotton or silk ribbons   Smaller sizes of cotton and silk ribbons can be used just like embroidery floss to give depth to a design. Also great for use in any width for decorative bows or ties. Available at local craft and fabric stores or through many online resources.

Beaded-Appliqué Swing Skirt

This skirt is a variation of the Reverse-Appliqué Swing Skirt on page 149. We dressed it up by changing its color to black and grey and adding beaded appliqué, one of our favorite techniques for fancier pieces. But you don't need to reserve beaded appliqué just for fancy garments; you can use it to draw attention to or add an additional layer of embellishment to any project. We often combine this technique with other types of beading—such as fade beading—which you can learn more about on page 31. Before you start this project, also check the tip on making a beading glove on page 99, which will make the actual beading process easier.

My Design Choices

Top fabric	– Dark grey
Backing fabric	– Black
Appliqué fabric	– Black
Fabric paint	– Grey
Thread	– Black
Beads	– #3 black bugle beads
Knots	– Positioned on skirt's wrong side

Supplies

Four extra-large cotton-jersey T-shirts *(two in one color for top layer and two in second color for backing layer)* or ³⁄₄ yard 60"-wide cotton jersey per color *(1¹⁄₂ yards total)*

One cotton-jersey T-shirt for rose appliqué

Skirt pattern *(see pattern sheet at back of book)*

Rose stencil *(see page 113)*

Paper scissors

Garment scissors

Embroidery scissors

Tailor's chalk or disappearing-ink pen

Tools needed for your choice of stencil-transfer method *(see page 28)*

³⁄₄ yard of 1"-wide fold-over elastic binding *(type used for diapers)*

Needle

Large-eyed millinery needle *(for beading)*

Pins

Buttonhole, carpet, and craft thread

All-purpose sewing thread

Approximately 1,100 bugle beads

1. Prepare Pattern and Stencil

Photocopy the skirt pattern, and use paper scissors to cut the photocopied pattern to your desired size (see page 53), cutting as close as possible to the black cutting line. If you're using T-shirts instead of yardage, lay the skirt's one pattern piece on top of each of your T-shirts before cutting to make sure that the T-shirts are long enough for the pattern's length (be sure to orient the pattern vertically on the T-shirt, so the pattern's marked grain line runs in the same direction as the fabric's grain

line [see page 48]). If the pattern doesn't fit, use larger T-shirts. The skirt's pattern has a ¹⁄₄" seam allowance built into its edges.

Photocopy the Rose stencil, enlarging it by 200 percent. Prepare and cut the stencil according to the instructions on page 58.

2. Deconstruct T-Shirts

If you're using yardage, skip to Step 3. If you're using T-shirts, deconstruct all four of them, as explained on page 48, so that each one is a sleeveless tube of fabric that's separated at the shoulder seams. Cut each tube into separate front and back panels by cutting from the bottom edge below the center of one armhole straight up to that center armhole and then repeating the process on the other side.

Prepare Pattern *(Step 1)*

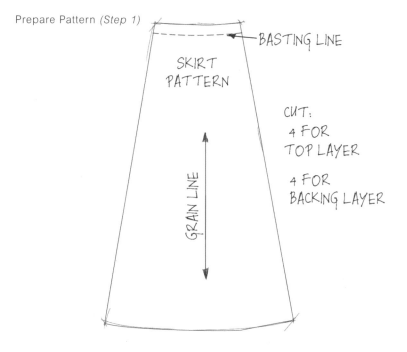

BASTING LINE

SKIRT PATTERN

GRAIN LINE

CUT:
4 FOR
TOP LAYER

4 FOR
BACKING LAYER

3. Cut Top-Layer Pattern Pieces

Decide which color of yardage or deconstructed T-shirt you want to use for the top layer of your skirt, and lay the skirt pattern on top of that yardage laid flat and single layer or on top of one of the T-shirt panels, making sure that the pattern's and T-shirt's grain lines run in the same direction. With tailor's chalk, trace around the pattern's edges, remove the pattern, and cut out the traced pattern, cutting just inside the chalked line. Repeat this step with the remaining yardage or T-shirt panels in the same color to get four top layers for your skirt. (If you want, you can lay one of the deconstructed T-shirts on top of another one, and cut out two fabric pieces at a time; but always make sure the grain lines on both fabrics run in the same direction.)

Cutting Top-Layer Pattern Pieces *(Step 3)*

4. Cut Backing-Layer Pattern Pieces

Lay out flat and single-layer the yardage or T-shirt fabric that you want to use as your backing fabric, and repeat the process in Step 3 to cut four full backing-layer pieces (using full panels as backing layers helps support the weight of the beaded appliqué). Note that you'll see the backing layer's color only at the skirt's hem, which is left a raw, unfinished edge.

5. Baste Waistlines

To ensure that the waistline on your cut fabric pieces doesn't stretch while you're working on your skirt, use a single strand of all-purpose thread to baste (see page 37) the edges of each of the waistlines on your cut pieces, as indicated on the pattern piece (see the illustration on the facing page).

6. Stencil Design on Top Layer

Place one of your top-layer panels on a covered work surface, with the fabric's right side (see page 48) facing up. Lay your Rose stencil (or a stencil of your choice) over the panel piece. Using your preferred stencil-transfer method, transfer the stencil on the top-layer panel along the skirt's bottom edge, moving the stencil and repeating the transfer as needed so that the design runs along the entire bottom edge. Repeat the stencil transfer on the remaining three top-layer panels.

7. Appliqué Rose Stencil

Lay your T-shirt for the Rose appliqué wrong side up on your work surface. Turn your Rose stencil to the wrong side, and position it on the appliqué fabric so that you'll have space for a second Rose stencil alongside the first (be sure the stencil is dry from the previous transfer before positioning it now). Using your choice of stencil-transfer method, transfer the stencil and let it dry. Repeat the stencil-transfer process on the second T-shirt panel to make a total of four stenciled Roses. Carefully cut out each individual petal of the transferred Rose stencils.

8. Prepare Cut Fabric for Stitching Panels

Center each top stenciled panel on top of a backing panel, with the right sides of both fabrics facing up; and pat the layers into place (see page 52) so that their edges are aligned. Pin the layers together securely.

9. Stitch Beaded Appliqué

Carefully align and pin each Rose petal appliqué, with the appliqué fabric's right side up, to a matching stenciled petal on one of the cut skirt panels. Thread your needle with a single strand of thread, "love" your thread (see page 21), and knot off (see page 40); then insert your needle from the wrong side of the skirt panel up to the top through the edge of one petal of the Rose appliqué. Add one bugle bead on your needle, and, using a whipstitch (see page 39), sew around the petal's edge, taking one bugle bead with each whipstitch. Knot off the thread on the fabric's wrong side when you arrive back where you started stitching. Then thread your needle again, move onto the next petal, and continue stitching around it with the beaded whipstitch. Continue stitching and following the guidelines for appliqué on page 62 until you've beaded and stitched around all the Rose petal appliqués. Avoid beading in the 1/4" seam allowance of each panel since the beads can make construction in Step 11 difficult; simply eliminate the bead in the 1/4" seam allowance and sew a regular whipstitch.

After completing all the Rose petal appliqués, appliqué the Rose stems using a standard whipstitch without beads to attach them.

10. Prepare for Construction

Once you've completed stitching and beading the top layer of your skirt, begin constructing the skirt by pinning together the seams of each pair of panels, with right sides together and using the instructions for "Felled Seams on the Wrong Side" on page 45.

11. Construct Skirt

Thread your needle, love your thread, and knot off. Using a straight stitch, begin stitching the pinned seams, bringing the needle up from the skirt's wrong side (so the knot shows on the inside), starting at the top edge of the skirt's waistline, and stitching 1/4" from the fabric's cut edges down to the bottom edge. Be sure to begin and end the seam by wrap-stitching (see page 45) its edges to keep it from pulling out later as you wear it. "Fell" your seam by folding the seam allowance to one side and topstitching the seam allowances 1/4" from the cut edges (that is, down the center of the seam allowances), using a straight stitch and wrap-stitching the beginning and end of the felled seam.

Repeat this process to stitch together all four skirt panels, checking the thread tension (see page 35), so the fabric lies flat along your seam before you knot off thread at end of seam.

12. Add Elastic to Waistline

Fold your elastic binding in half; and, starting and ending at the center-back waistline, pin the elastic to the skirt's waistline, overlapping the waistline's cut edge, so the elastic acts as a binding that finishes that edge. Overlap the cut ends of the elastic where they meet for a clean look.

We stitched the elastic binding in place with the zigzag stitch (see page 38), but any stretchable stitch will work. Thread your needle, love your thread, and knot off. Starting at the center back, where the ends of your elastic overlap, insert your needle from the skirt's wrong side, bringing it out on the right side; and zigzag-stitch all the way around the skirt to attach the elastic binding. Finally knot off on the skirt's wrong side.

Note: The skirt's hem is left as a raw, unfinished edge.

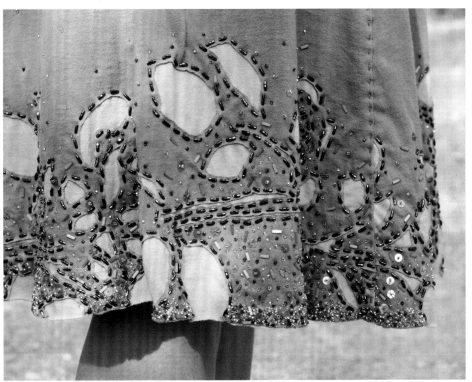

Adding On

I made the dress above some years ago. It's similar to this skirt project, except I used beaded reverse appliqué for the roses and leaves. This dress is a favorite of mine, and I continue to stitch and embellish it as time goes by. When I have time, I like to sit and stitch and think, continuing to add beads and other elements at my whim. I think of it as a work in progress; and with each stitch, it just becomes more beautiful. Any of the projects in this book can be embellished over time in the same way.

Sampler Quilt

A few years ago my colleagues made me a quilt that used every stencil that I'd ever designed and finished it with a handwritten personal message. This special gesture was very touching, and it actually has a long tradition in American quilting history, especially in the nineteenth century when women often made friendship quilts. These quilts were worked from individual blocks designed by friends and family, so pioneer women who were moving away could take a little part of their old life with them.

Like my beautiful quilt, friendship quilts are similar to scrapbooks because they can contain poetry, autographs, and special messages. I cried on the day I received my quilt, and it's a prized possession that marks the passage of people and time. Their hard work and dedication will always be a part of my life, with the memories stored in that quilt for eternity.

This project pays homage to every person who has stitched, worked for, or been a part of the birth of Alabama Chanin. It uses all the stencils featured in previous projects in this book and offers a great way to practice your skills. Make it all at once or one block at a time over a longer period.

My Design Choices

Top fabric   - White
Backing fabric   - Bleached blue
Appliqué fabric   - Bleached blue
Paint   - Tan
Thread   - Tan
Knots   - Positioned on top fabric's right side

Supplies

Twenty cotton-jersey T-shirts, ten in one color and ten in second color, or 1½ yards of 60"-wide cotton jersey in each color *(3 yards total)*

12" square of pattern paper *(see page 23 for paper options)*

Lace Stripe stencil, enlarged 300 percent *(see page 78)*

Rooster stencil, enlarged 455 percent *(see page 88)*

Bloomers stencil *(see pullout)*

Rose stencil, enlarged 200 percent *(see page 113)*

Garment scissors

Embroidery scissors

Transparent plastic ruler

Tailor's chalk or disappearing-ink fabric pen

Tools for your choice of stencil-transfer method *(see page 28)*

Pins

Needle

Buttonhole, carpet, and craft thread

Finished Dimensions

Approximately 48" x 60"

Prepare Pattern *(Step 1)*

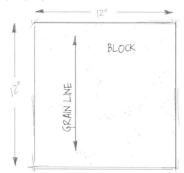

1. Prepare Pattern and Stencils

On your 12" square of pattern paper, draw a line parallel to one side, and label this line "Grain Line" and the rectangle itself "Block" (see below). Photocopy and enlarge stencils as indicated in Supplies list. Prepare and cut stencils according to instructions on page 58.

2. Prepare Fabric for Cutting

If you're using T-shirts instead of yardage, deconstruct all twenty of them as explained on page 48 so that each one is a sleeveless tube of fabric that's separated at the shoulder seams. Then cut each T-shirt tube from the bottom edge below the center of one armhole straight up to that center armhole so that the tube lies flat as a single layer. The fabric used to cut blocks for the backing layer on my quilt was lightly bleached. If you want to similarly treat your fabric, see the directions for bleaching on page 89, and prepare the fabric for the blocks on the quilt back now. If not, go on to the next step.

3. Cut Out Pattern Pieces

Place the Block pattern piece on top of one deconstructed T-shirt or the yardage that you've laid flat and single-layer, making sure that the pattern's marked grain line and the fabric's grain line (see page 48) run in the same direction. With tailor's chalk, carefully trace around the pattern's edges, remove the pattern, and cut out the block, cutting just inside the chalked line to remove all the chalk. Repeat this step on the remaining panels or yardage of the first color to get twenty blocks in that color. Then, using the panels from the second color of deconstructed T-shirts or the other yardage, repeat this step to get twenty blocks in the second color, for a total of forty blocks in two colors.

4. Stencil Design on Quilt Top

Using the illustration at top left on the facing page as a guide and your stencil-transfer method of choice (see page 28), transfer

Stencil Design on Quilt Top *(Step 4)*

each stencil design to your blocks, making sure each time before stenciling that the right side (see page 48) of the fabric block faces up.

5. Embellish and Construct Blocks

Using the chart at right as a guide for your treatment of each block, embellish and construct each one. You'll find instructions for appliqué on page 62, for reverse appliqué on page 64, and for 3-D appliqué on page 66. Note that we chose to place our knots on the top layer of each block, so they're visible on the completed quilt.

6. Sew Blocks Together

Start by laying out the first horizontal row of blocks and pin the edges of each pair of blocks, with wrong sides together (you'll be

Embellish and Construct Blocks *(Step 5)*

APPLIQUÉ LACE STRIPE	REVERSE APPLIQUÉ ROSE	3-D ROSE	REVERSE APPLIQUÉ LACE STRIPE
3-D ROOSTER	REVERSE APPLIQUÉ LACE STRIPE	3-D BLOOMERS	REVERSE APPLIQUÉ ROSE
APPLIQUÉ BLOOMERS	REVERSE APPLIQUÉ ROOSTER	REVERSE APPLIQUÉ LACE STRIPE	REVERSE APPLIQUÉ BLOOMERS
3-D LACE STRIPE	APPLIQUÉ ROSE	REVERSE APPLIQUÉ BLOOMERS	REVERSE APPLIQUÉ ROSE
APPLIQUÉ BLOOMERS	REVERSE APPLIQUÉ ROSE	REVERSE APPLIQUÉ LACE STRIPE	APPLIQUÉ ROOSTER

seaming the blocks together with what we call floating seams on the right side, meaning your seam allowances will be visible on the outside of the quilt (see page 43). Thread your needle, "love" your thread (see page 21), knot off (see page 40), and seam the individual blocks together with a straight stitch (see page 36), wrap-stitching (see page 45) the beginning and end of each seam. Continue pinning and seaming together each horizontal row of blocks, and then pin and seam the five horizontal rows together.

7. Finish Edges

Starting in the middle of one side (instead of at a corner, which is always a little harder to handle), use the parallel whipstitch (see page 39) or blanket stitch to finish the entire outside edge of your quilt.

Acknowledgments

Aaron & Christine Smith, Stanley & Lucille Perkins, Billy & Sherry Smith, Zach Chanin, Butch Anthony & Maggie Anthony-Chanin, Jennifer & Robert Rausch, Lisa & Jess Morphew & Fish Film, Myra & Jim Brown, Joy Kelly, Diane Hall, Erin Dempsey, Eva Whitechapel, Elaine Poorman, Steven Smith, Sissi Farassat, Jennifer Venditti, Gayle Dizon, Lori Goldstein, Sara Martin, Sergej Schmeid, George & La Donna Perkins, Michael Pause, Igor & Gammon, Eric Kosse, Peter Stangelmayr & Avena, Judith Eisler, Ashli Kennedy, Jessica Bartlett, Melanie Falick, Stacie Stukin, Birgit Burtelmair, Mag Rhodes, Annalee Bloomfield, Thom Driver, Angie Moser, Chris Timmons, Southern Foodways Alliance, Alabama State Council for the Arts, Shoals Community in Northwest Alabama, Lisa Fox, Paul Graves & other former business partners, our stitchers, supporters, all of those who have believed, & many, many more....

Photographer - Elizabeth DeRamus

Natalie Chanin, former costume designer and fashion stylist, is the founder and head designer of Alabama Chanin. She has been featured in *Vogue, Time, The New York Times*, and on CBS News. In 2006 she was selected for membership by the Council of Fashion Designers of America. Her work has also been recognized by the CFDA/Vogue Fashion Fund, the Cooper-Hewitt National Design Museum, the Alabama Council for the Arts, and Aid to Artisans, among others.

To learn more about Alabama Chanin, visit www.alabamachanin.com.

Published in 2008 by Stewart, Tabori & Chang
An imprint of Harry N. Abrams, Inc.

Library of Congress Cataloging-in-Publication Data

Chanin, Natalie.
Alabama stitch book : projects and stories celebrating hand-sewing, quilting, and embroidery for contemporary sustainable style /
by Natalie Chanin with Stacie Stukin ; photography by Robert Rausch.
p. cm.
Includes index.
ISBN 978-1-58479-638-1
1. Cross-stitch. I. Title.
TT778.C76C43 2008
746.44'304109761--dc22
2007019269

Printed and bound in China
10 9 8 7 6 5 4 3 2 1

Editor: Melanie Falick
Technical Editor: Chris Timmons
Designer: Robert Rausch
Production Manager: Jacquie Poirier

HNA
harry n. abrams, inc.
a subsidiary of La Martinière Groupe

115 West 18th Street,
New York, NY 10011
www.hnabooks.com